CONTENTS

Appetizers

Brunch

Soups

Salads & Vegetables

Main Dishes

Desserts

Introduction

* * * * *

This recipe book is for all who love, laugh, cry, enjoy, and applaud life. Today we wear our tiaras and stand tall for "Our Moment In Tiara Time." We relish our own uniqueness, we celebrate life, we're proud of every cherished laugh line, we praise each gray hair earned through life's lessons that have been peppered and woven throughout our tresses, and we are acutely aware of each new ache and pain we never imagined possible. Shhhh!!!! Not to mention those extra pounds we swore we were never going to gain!

Within this book you will find time treasured recipes that I've enjoyed savoring and serving over the past 35 years while entertaining old friends, family and new friends at Teacups & Tiaras. It will be my pleasure to have you enjoy this collection. Remember, everyday is your party, you capture your spirit, you enjoy the lifestyle of celebration and you continue your journey to seize the spirit of your uniqueness.

With life's many facets, just like the jewels in our tiaras, we come to an age, stage, and faze in time that captures our essence and defines ourselves. I seize today by plucking every moment of yesterday's knowledge and combining it with freedom, independence, attitude, and gusto so that tomorrow I will be all that I can be.

A little place sent from heaven has been created here on earth to capture and relive past childhood memories. Teacups & Tiaras is an uplifting, fun, and entertaining experience for children of all ages. Whether you don a tiara or hat, you can enjoy the child within for a moment in time, while being waited on and pampered in a creative and pleasurable atmosphere. We hope your senses will been heightened, your heart delighted, and your imagination has taken flight during your visit.

Happy Wand Waving To You ~Until We Meet Again

Connie

*Age is something
that doesn't matter,
unless you are a cheese
~Billie Burke*

Roquefort Terrine

* * * * *

*No matter what your age or dress size, this is
sure to delight your taste buds!!*

6 Oz.	Roquefort – crumbled
1 Stick	Unsalted butter
¼ C + 1Tbs.	Chopped walnuts – toasted
2 Tsp.	Ground pepper

Puree ½ cheese + butter in food processor and transfer to a mixing bowl. Fold in remaining cheese, ¼ cup of the nuts and pepper. Chill 2 hours on a serving dish of choice.

Before serving, soften to room temperature for 30 minutes and sprinkle with remaining nuts. Serve on toasted baguette slices.

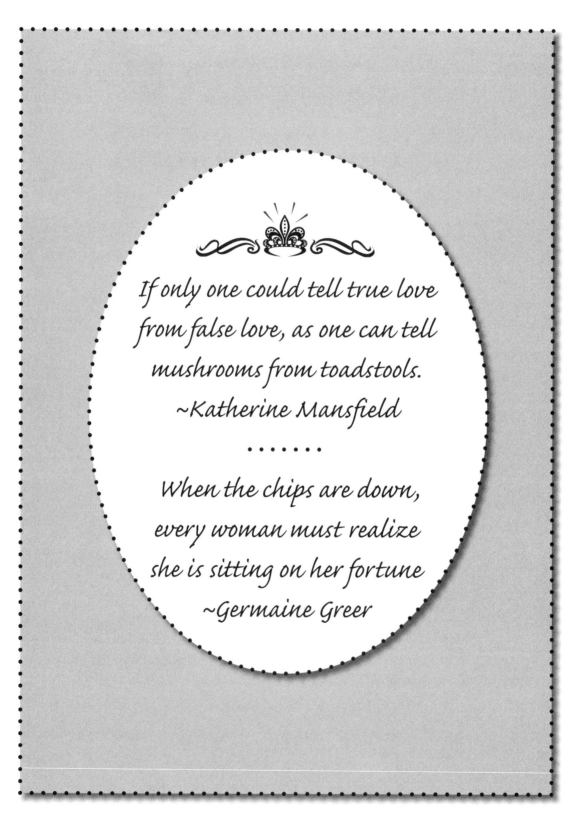

If only one could tell true love from false love, as one can tell mushrooms from toadstools.
~Katherine Mansfield

. . . .

When the chips are down, every woman must realize she is sitting on her fortune
~Germaine Greer

Wild Mushroom Pate'

* * * * *

*Take this to the next office gathering. You'll be as wild
as the pate' and the "love" of the party!*

½	Cup walnuts – toasted	1	Tbs. fresh thyme
6	Tbs. butter – unsalted	6	Scallions – white & pale
8	Oz. cream cheese		green chopped
1	Tsp. lemon juice	1 ¾	Lb.'s mushrooms
¼	Cup parsley – fresh		(approx. 7 cups) – chopped
⅓	Cup Madeira wine		(use cremini, shiitake,
1	Tsp. pepper		portobello, & white button)
1 ½	Tsp. salt	14-16	Button mushrooms for garnish

Line a 3 cup mold with plastic wrap and then spray the plastic wrap with cooking oil. Blend in a food processor the butter, cream cheese, lemon juice, parsley, Madeira wine, thyme, salt, pepper, and scallions. Fold in the walnuts and mushrooms.

Fill the mold and refrigerate 8 hours or overnight. Unmold on serving plate, garnish with mushrooms, fresh thyme sprigs, and pepper strips. Serve with peppered crackers.

Zucchini Madeleine

* * * * *

Those French have all the fun – try it you'll like it – a true tickler!

1	Cup zucchini – shredded, salted & drained at least 1 hour in colander	10	Eggs – beaten
		¾	Cup oil
		½	Cup Parmesan cheese – fresh
1	Large onion – chopped	1 ½	Tsp. pepper
1	Garlic clove – minced	2	Cup biscuit mix

Grease and flour madeleine pans. In a large bowl combine the drained zucchini, chopped onion, garlic, eggs, oil, cheese, pepper and biscuit mix. Mix well and spoon into prepared madeleine pans. Bake in a 350 oven for 20-25 minutes. Serve with shrimp sauce.

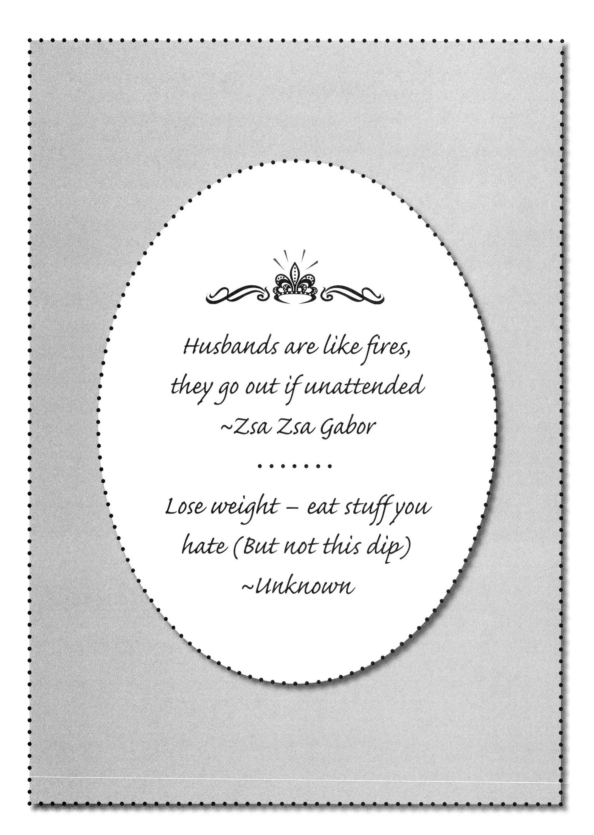

Husbands are like fires,
they go out if unattended
~Zsa Zsa Gabor

. . . .

Lose weight – eat stuff you
hate (But not this dip)
~Unknown

Black Bean Salsa

* * * * *

Men love this one! Ole' – You just hit a home run.

1	Can black beans – drained & rinsed	1	Jar salsa (thick & chunky)
1	Can Mexican corn – drained	1	Can black olives – sliced
1	Medium red onion	1	Green pepper – chopped
		1	8 Oz. pkg. shredded cheddar cheese

Mix all ingredients, chill, and serve with tortilla chips.

Roasted Red Pepper Dip

* * * * *

He'll be chasing you around the kitchen table – you red hot mama!

2	Large red bell peppers roasted – peeled & seeded (may substitute 4 oz. jar of roasted red peppers)	1-2	Pickled jalapeno peppers – chopped
		¼	Cup cilantro – chopped
4	Oz. sundried tomatoes packed in oil – patted dry	1	Bunch green onions – whites only
2	Garlic cloves	6	Oz. Cream cheese
2	Tsp. ground cumin	½	Tsp. Salt

Place roasted, peeled and seeded red peppers in a food processor. Add sundried tomatoes, garlic, ground cumin, chopped pickled peppers, cilantro, green onions, cream cheese and salt. Blend to combine.

Remove to serving dish and chill. Serve with pita points.

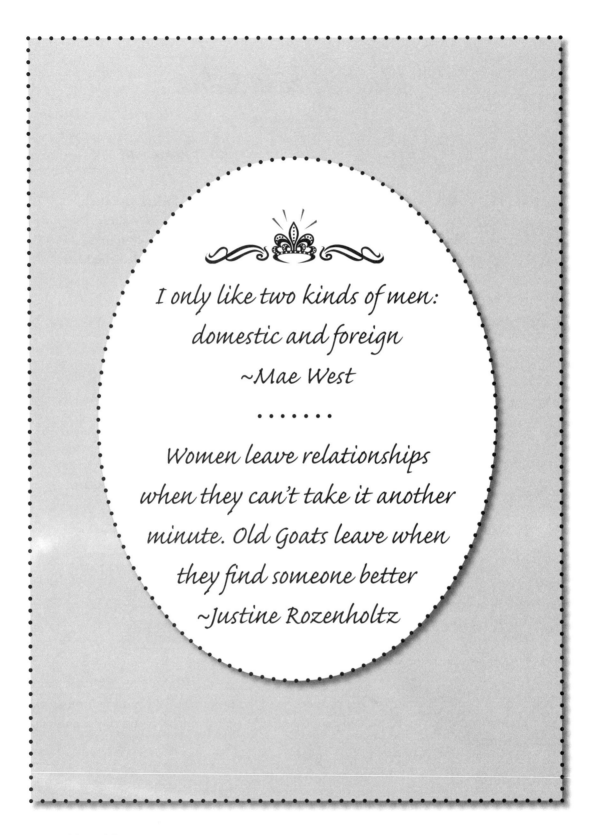

*I only like two kinds of men:
domestic and foreign
~Mae West*

. . . .

*Women leave relationships
when they can't take it another
minute. Old Goats leave when
they find someone better
~Justine Rozenholtz*

Hot Crab

* * * * *

You won't have any "Crabby" guests at your
next party when this is served.

1	Lb. crab meat – fresh, or good Krabby (OK)	2	8 Oz. whipped cream cheese
1	Can fancy white crabmeat	5-6	Green onions – chopped
2	Cup mayo		

Chop crab meat to medium dice. Drain fancy white crab meat and add to chopped meat. Combine mayo, softened whipped cream cheese and green onions (whites only) with crab. Place in baking dish, sprinkle with slivered almonds and paprika.

Bake at 350 for 20-30 minutes. Serve hot with toast points or water crackers.

Goat Cheese Baguette

* * * * *

This is so delicious that the 'Old Goat' or 'Old Coot'
in your life will adore you.

1	French bread baguette – cut into ¼" slices	¼	Cup sundried tomatoes – oil packed & patted dry
¾	Cup ripe tomatoes – seeded & diced	2	Tbs. fresh basil – chopped
		¾	Oz. log goat cheese – plain

Place sliced bread on cookie sheet and bake for 5 minutes in 350 oven. Remove and top with goat cheese. Mix the seeded and diced tomatoes, the sundried tomatoes, and chopped basil together. Place on top of goat cheese and give a good grind of black pepper. Return to oven and bake for 3-5 minutes more.

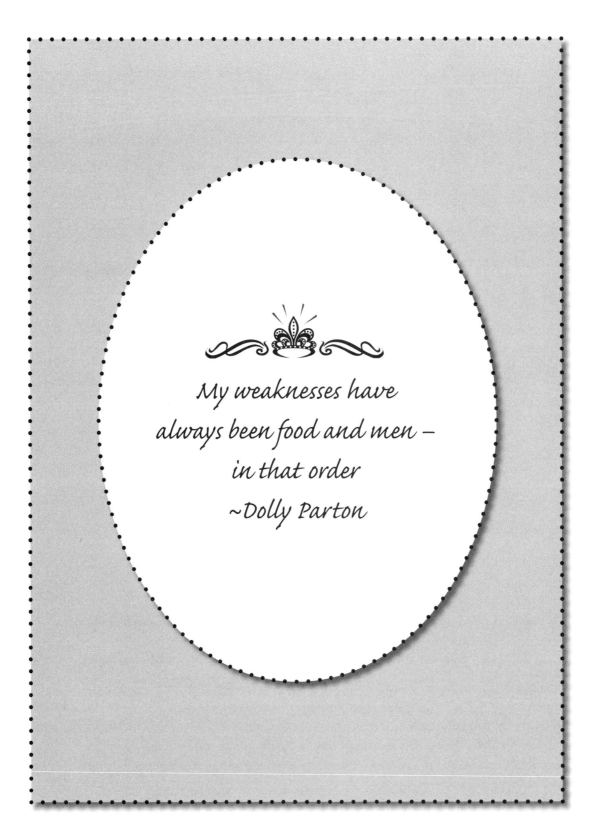

My weaknesses have
always been food and men –
in that order
~Dolly Parton

Mushroom Tart

* * * * *

When was the last time you had a tart? They're not all sweet, some are savory. Ooooh, and here are two of my favorites – Yummy!!!

Pastry Shells: Separate 2 cans of butterflake rolls. Grease mini muffin pans. Separate each roll into 2 parts. Flatten and press into pan. Bake at 375- 400 for 10-12 minutes or until brown.

A. Mushroom Filling:

1	Lb. mushrooms – finely chopped	½	Cup flour
4	Tbs. green onion – minced	1	Tsp. Salt
½	Cup butter	2	Cup whipping cream

Sauté mushrooms and green onions in butter. Blend in flour and salt. Add cream and continue cooking over medium heat until thick and smooth. Fill pastry shells. Bake at 375 for 12 -15 minutes.

B. Sausage Filling:

1	Lb. sausage	¼	Tsp. pepper
1	Small onion – chopped	¼	Lb. mushrooms
½	Cup milk	1	egg
½	Tsp. salt	½	Cup shredded cheddar

Brown sausage (I prefer Jimmy Dean Sage) with onion and mushrooms. Beat egg and milk together and add to the sausage, onion, and mushroom mixture. Add cheese, salt and pepper. Mix all ingredients well. Fill shells heaping full with tablespoon. Bake in oven at 350 for 15-20 minutes.

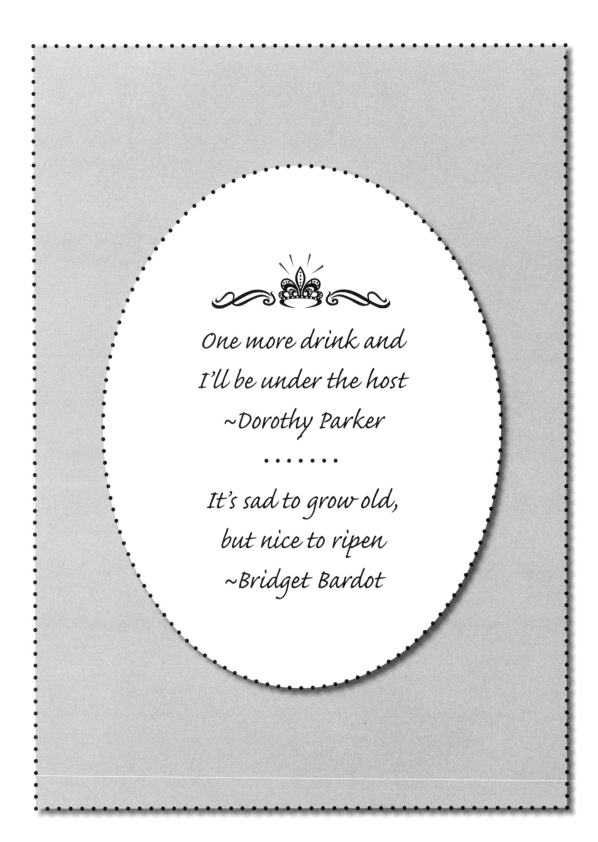

One more drink and
I'll be under the host
~Dorothy Parker

. . . .

It's sad to grow old,
but nice to ripen
~Bridget Bardot

Cocktail Rye

* * * * *

These are "top of the table" dancin' good !!

1 Lb.	Sausage (Jimmy Dean) – plain
1 ½ Lb.	Velveeta cheese
1 Bottle	Chili sauce (Del Monte)
1 Pkg.	Cocktail rye bread

Brown sausage and add cheese. Reduce heat and continue to cook until cheese melts and becomes bubbly. Open chili sauce and spread 1 Tbs. of the sauce onto each rye square. Place on cookie sheet and top with sausage/cheese mixture. Bake at 350 for 15-20 minutes or until cheese bubbles.

Apricot Brie

* * * * *

Put fruit and cheese together and my wish list is complete.

½ C	Apricot jam
1 Tbs.	Grated orange peel
1 Tbs.	Orange juice
1 Tbs.	Lemon juice
⅛ Tsp.	Cinnamon
1 -8 Oz.	Wedge of Brie

Mix jam, orange peel, orange juice, lemon juice, and cinnamon in shallow dish large enough to hold Brie when added later. Heat sauce in microwave until it begins to bubble. Set Brie in sauce. Return to microwave and cook until Brie is warm and slightly melted. Check every 20 seconds; serve with crackers or baguette slices.

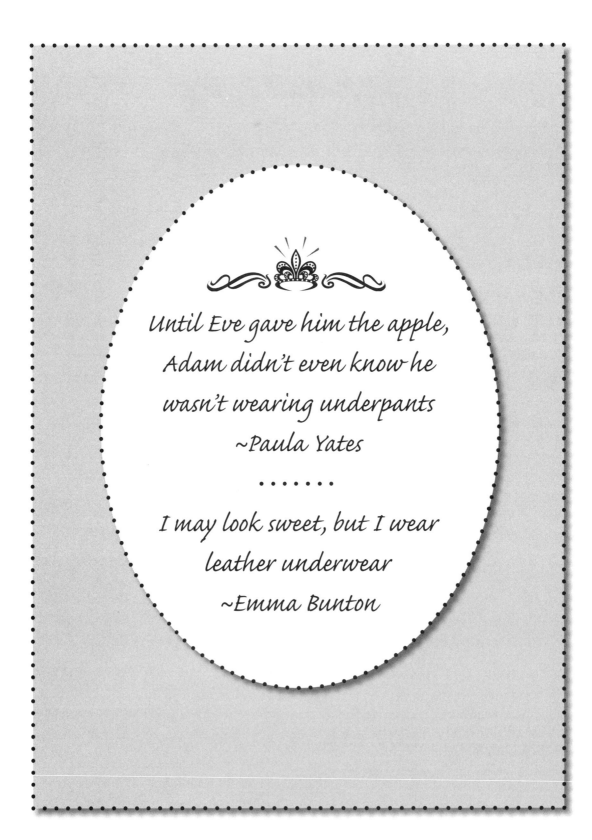

Until Eve gave him the apple, Adam didn't even know he wasn't wearing underpants
~Paula Yates

. . . .

I may look sweet, but I wear leather underwear
~Emma Bunton

Apple/Berry Salsa

* * * * *

If it's good enough for Adam, it's good enough for my "Honey."

2	Granny Smith apples	2	Tbs. brown sugar – light
1	Kiwi	2	Tbs. apple jelly
1	Cup strawberries		

Chop all fruit and mix together with jelly and brown sugar. Serve with Cinnamon Chips.

Cinnamon Chips: Cut flour tortillas into triangles. Place on baking sheet and sprinkle with cinnamon/sugar mixture. Bake for 5-10 minutes in a 300 oven.

Pears with Boursin Cheese

* * * * *

A little spicier, a little creamier, and aaaah it's delectable.

8	Oz. cream cheese softened to room temperature	1	Garlic clove – finely chopped
2	Tbs. mayo	1	Tsp. dill – finely chopped
1	Tsp. Dijon mustard	1 ½	Tsp. Parmesan cheese
1 ½	Tsp. chives – finely chopped		Pinch cayenne pepper
		6	Fresh or canned pears patted dry

Blend cheese with mixer until smooth and creamy. Add the remaining ingredients and mix together well. Transfer mixture to container and refrigerate for 48 hours.

To plate, wash pears (fresh) and cut in half. Scoop out center with melon baller. Fill each pear half with 1 Tbs. of cheese mixture. Serve chilled.

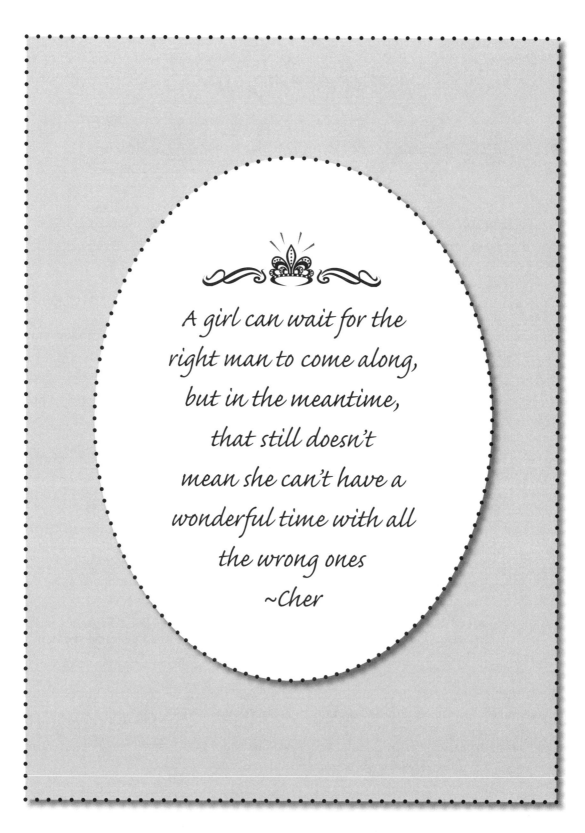

A girl can wait for the
right man to come along,
but in the meantime,
that still doesn't
mean she can't have a
wonderful time with all
the wrong ones
~Cher

Caviar Pie

* * * * *

I'd love to be an egg farm if mine were worth $250 an ounce.
Who wouldn't want to lounge around all day just waiting
to be puffed on a pillow of sour cream.

12	Eggs – hard boiled
½ C	Butter
3 Tsp.	Prepared mustard
½ Tsp.	Salt
¼ Tsp.	Pepper
2 Tsp.	Cider vinegar
1 C	Green onions – chopped
¾ C	Sour Cream
10 Oz.	Cream cheese
4 Tbs.	Pimiento – chopped
	Red caviar
	Black caviar
	Pumpernickel toast

In a food processor combine the eggs, butter, mustard, salt, pepper, and vinegar until smooth. Spread on the bottom of a buttered 8-inch spring form pan. Sprinkle with onions. Refrigerate at least 1 hour. Combine the sour cream, cream cheese, and pimiento in the food processor until smooth. Layer on top. Refrigerate for at least 1 hour. When ready to serve, cut into 16 wedges and top with 1 Tsp. each of red and black caviar. Serve with pumpernickel toast slices.

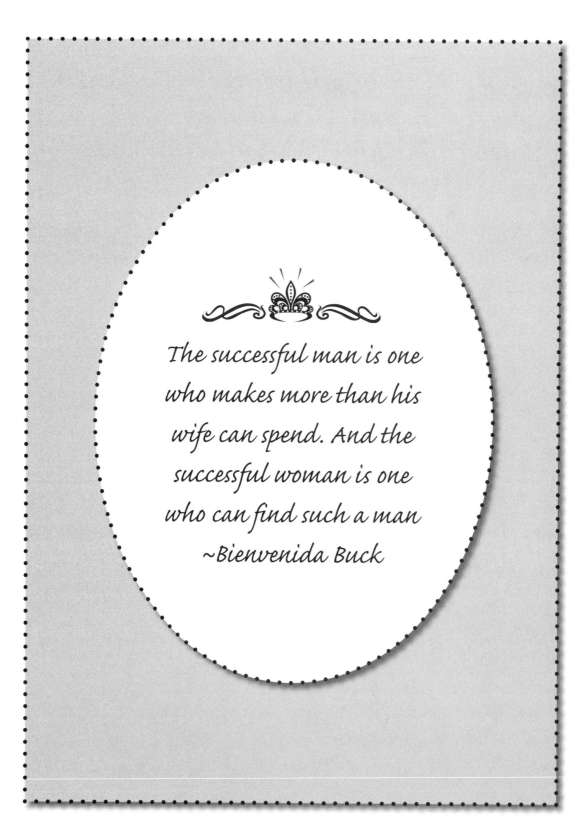

The successful man is one who makes more than his wife can spend. And the successful woman is one who can find such a man
~Bienvenida Buck

Brunch Enchiladas

* * * * *

*Just look at these ingredients – what's not to like,
just put them together & voila!!!*

12 Oz.	Cooked Ham – ground
½ C	Green onions – sliced
½ C	Green pepper – chopped
2 ½ C	Cheddar cheese – shredded
8	7" flour tortillas
4	Eggs – beaten
2 C	Half & Half
1 Tbs.	Flour
¼ Tsp.	Salt
¼ Tsp.	Garlic powder
2-3 Dashes	Hot pepper sauce

In bowl: Combine ham, onion and pepper. Place ⅓ C of this mixture and 3 Tbs. of cheese at one end of each tortilla and roll up. Place seam side down in 9x12 greased baking dish.

In a mixing bowl combine eggs, cream, flour, salt, garlic, and hot pepper sauce. Pour over tortilla rolls, cover and refrigerate several hours.

Bake uncovered at 350 for 45-50 minutes. Sprinkle with remaining cheese and bake 3-5 minutes more. Let stand for 10 minutes.

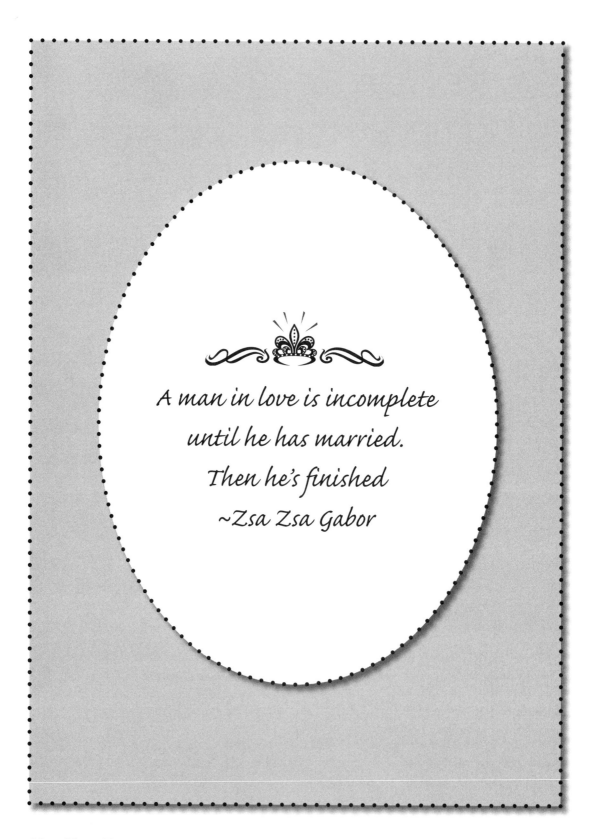

A man in love is incomplete
until he has married.
Then he's finished
~Zsa Zsa Gabor

Scrambled Eggs & Wild Rice in Phyllo Cups

* * * * *

The First Lady of Iowa, Christie Vilsack, brought other Governor's wives to the Tearoom for a breakfast and this was served. Simple, yet elegant!

¼	Cup onion – sliced		Salt & pepper to taste
6	Eggs	1	Tbs. tarragon
1	Tbs. Half & Half	1	Tbs. parsley – chopped
½	Tbs. butter	¼	Cup wild rice – prepared

Sauté onion in butter until translucent. Beat eggs with Half & Half. Add egg mixture to onion and complete cooking. Add wild rice, salt and pepper to taste.

Phyllo Cups: Thaw phyllo dough to room temperature and cut sheets into quarters. Spray each sheet of dough with cooking oil and place in a cupcake size muffin tin. Sprinkle each sheet with herbs and layer four sheets over lapping each other per tin. While working with each four sheets, place remainder of dough under damp towel to prevent drying. Bake at 375 for 8-10 minutes or until cups are browned. When cool, remove from muffin tins and store in an airtight container.

To assemble: Arrange phyllo cups on cookie sheet or back into the muffin pan. Fill with egg and wild rice mixture. Top with diced tomato and jack cheese. Bake at 350 for 6-8 minutes until cheese melts and eggs are heated through. Makes 6 regular size muffin cups.

I have food dreams

instead of sex dreams

~Rona Jaffe

French Toast

* * * * *

In my family this has been called "orgasm french toast"
since the first taste.

2 C	Brown sugar (I always prefer dark)
1 ⅓ C	Margarine
4 Tbs.	Karo syrup
1 Tsp.	Cinnamon

Combine brown sugar, margarine, and Karo syrup in sauce pan and bring to boil. Once the brown sugar is dissolved, remove from heat and add cinnamon. Pour into 9x12 glass baking dish.

Place two layers of whole wheat bread on top of the cinnamon and sugar mixture. Gently press bread down to soak up some of the syrup sauce.

Mix:

5	Eggs
1 ½ C	Half & Half
1 Tbs.	Vanilla

Pour over bread and refrigerate overnight.

Set casserole out in the morning for 1 hour at room temperature. Bake at 350 for 45 to 60 minutes or until puffy and lightly browned. Invert onto serving platter or lined cookie sheet and serve immediately with sour cream and strawberries.

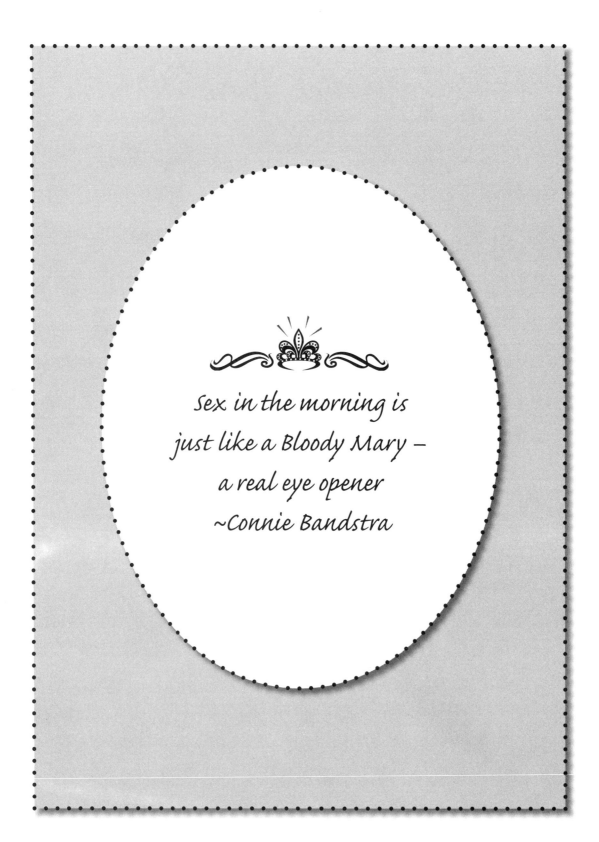

Sex in the morning is
just like a Bloody Mary –
a real eye opener
~Connie Bandstra

Ham & Egg Casserole

* * * * *

Dr. Seuss would even tip his top hat to this.

8	Eggs – boiled hard, shells removed
½ C	Butter – softened
1 Tsp.	Parsley – minced
1 Tbs.	Onion – grated
⅓ C	Boiled ham – grated

After removing shells from the hard boiled eggs, halve them and place yolks in a medium sized mixing bowl. Add softened butter, parsley, onion and ham. Combine until mixed thoroughly. Stuff egg white halves generously with mixture and arrange in greased baking dish. Cover with Béchamel Sauce.

Béchamel Sauce:

3 Tbs.	Butter
4 Tbs.	Flour
1 Cube	Beef bouillon
1 C	Boiling water
¾ C	Half & Half
1 C	American cheese – grated

Blend butter and flour together and slowly add boiling water. Add beef cube and continue stirring until smooth. Season with salt, pepper and paprika. Add Half & Half and continue to cook, stirring constantly, until thick.

Pour sauce over eggs and cover with grated American cheese. Bake at 300 for 30-40 minutes. Can be made the day ahead, however, make certain all ingredients are cooled.

I'm miserable if I'm not in
love and, of course,
I'm miserable if I am
~Tallulah Bankhead

German Apple Pancake

* * * * *

When he asks "Can we go for seconds, please" –
is that music to your ears or what?

3	Whole eggs
3	Eggs – separated
½ C + 2 Tbs.	Sugar
1 Tbs.	Vanilla
2 ¼ C	Whole milk
4 C	Flour
7	Granny Smith or Pippin apples – peeled & cored
7 Tbs	Butter
	Cinnamon sugar
	Sour cream, jam or marmalade

Mix whole eggs, egg yolks, sugar, vanilla, and milk until thoroughly combined. Stir in flour and mix well. Let stand 15 minutes. Whip the 3 egg whites in a separate bowl until stiff and fold into batter.

Cut 1 apple into ½ inch slices and sauté in 1 Tbs. of butter in a heavy stainless steel skillet until both sides are lightly browned having been turned frequently. Add 1 C batter, cover with lid and cook until golden brown underneath. Flip over and heat quickly until set. Sprinkle top with cinnamon sugar.

Place under broiler to brown. Slide pancake from skillet onto serving plate. Sprinkle with additional cinnamon sugar mixture.

Repeat process with remaining apples, butter and batter, cooking each pancake separately.

Serve with sour cream and/or jam. Makes 7 pancakes.

Cinnamon/Sugar: Mix 1 C sugar with 1 Tbs. ground cinnamon.

Once a woman has forgiven her man, she must not reheat his sins for breakfast
~Marlene Dietrich

Quiche

* * * * *

*I'm giving you the basics for this so get in the groove
and let your imaginations gooooooo!!!*

I have a standard procedure for making quiche. I use a 10 inch spring form pan. This eliminates the chore of removing a slice of pie from a tin and loosing it in the process. Plan on 8 generous slices out of each pie.

Basic recipe:

10	**Whole eggs**
2 C	**Whipping cream**

Additions: This is where you can let your imagination go.

- **Chili grind hamburger meat with caramelized onions, green pepper and Jack cheese**
- **Canadian bacon with wild rice, onions, thinly sliced tomatoes, Swiss, and Jack cheese**
- **Broccoli, pimento, and cheddar cheese (use lemon pepper for the sparkle in flavor)**
- **Ham and Asparagus with Swiss and Jack cheese**
- **Mediterranean with Artichoke hearts, sundried tomatoes, black olives and mushrooms combining Asiago, Parmesan, and Romano cheeses**
- **Spinach, chicken poached in rosemary, with Swiss and Jack cheese**

Again your seasonings will depend on your individual taste. Always remember not to over salt the custard as the cheeses do contain an abundance.

Quiche Crust: I always use puff pastry. Naturally, the Tearoom buys sheets from a bakery supply company. However, on occasion I have run out and was forced to buy the popular store brand and it works!!! Using that; thaw and roll in a circle on a slightly floured surface. Spray spring form pan with cooking spray and work pastry sheet into pan and up sides. Pastry sheet will not spill over the pan. Add quiche ingredients and bake at 350 for 60 minutes to 75 minutes or until quiche is firm.

I like to bake the quiche a day in advance of serving so the flavors meld.

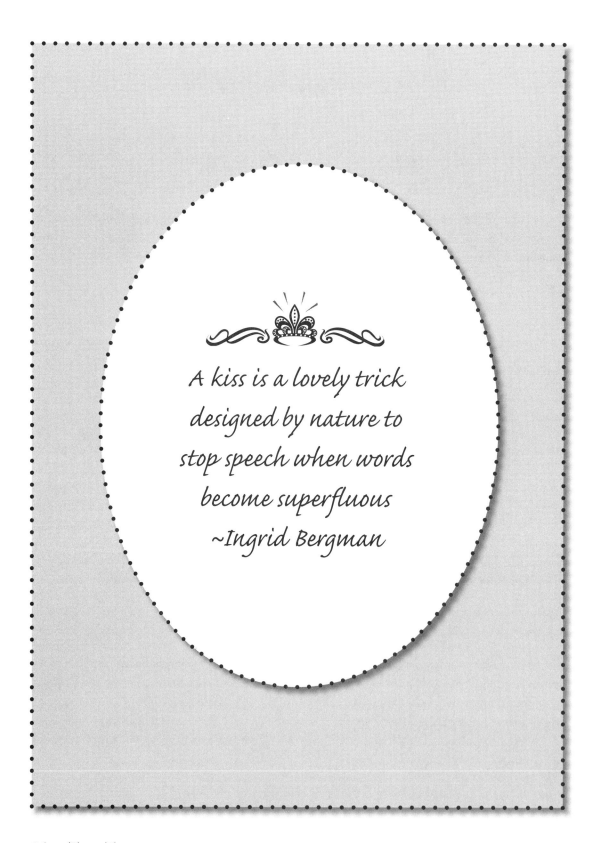

A kiss is a lovely trick
designed by nature to
stop speech when words
become superfluous
~Ingrid Bergman

French Toast Soufflé

* * * * *

With all of these exquisite ingredients, this has the elements of a quintessential morning winner.

9 Lg.	Croissants – torn coarsely
18 Lg.	Eggs
1 ½ C	Maple syrup
4 ½ C	Half & Half
1 C	Butter – room temperature
1 Tbs.	Cinnamon – plus additional for sprinkling
12 Oz.	Cream cheese
Garnish:	1 Cup chopped pecans
	Dusting of powdered sugar

Spray 16, 3-inch soufflé dishes with cooking spray. Put the torn croissants into the food processor and whirl until chopped to about walnut size. Divide equally into the soufflé dishes.

Using a blender, make the egg mixture in two batches (it will overflow otherwise). Whirl together ½ the eggs, maple syrup, Half & Half, butter and cinnamon, until well mixed, about 30 seconds. Add half the cream cheese and blend until mixture is smooth. Pour into a large bowl. Repeat the blender process with the remaining ingredients. Pour into large bowl and stir so both batches are combined completely. Pour over croissants in dishes, dividing equally. Sprinkle with additional cinnamon. Cover and refrigerate overnight or for at least 8 hours.

Preheat oven to 375. Remove dishes from refrigerator and place on cookie sheet; bake uncovered for 45-50 minutes. Remove and sprinkle with chopped pecans and dust with powdered sugar. Pass warm maple syrup.

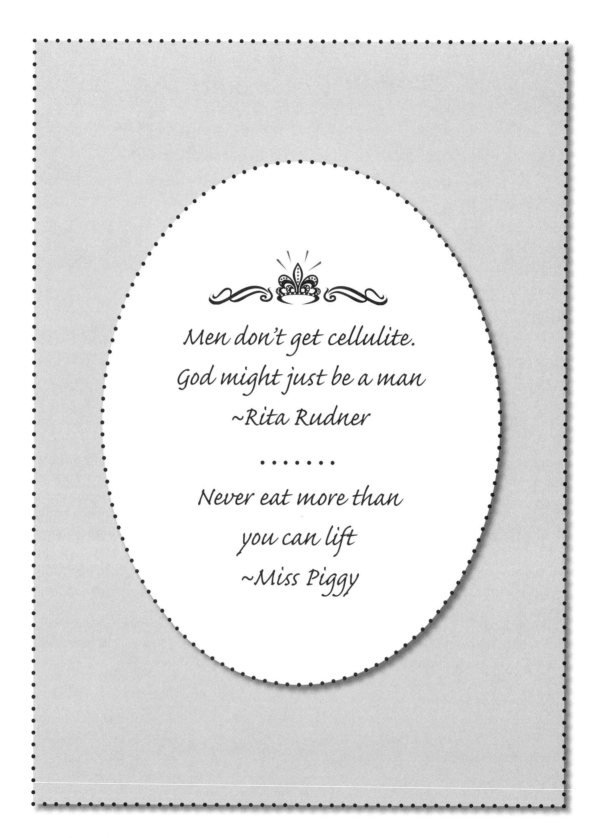

Men don't get cellulite.
God might just be a man
~Rita Rudner

· · · · · · ·

Never eat more than
you can lift
~Miss Piggy

Baked Blintzes

* * * * *

A friend and I got blitzed drinking Chambord
and Champagne while making this!!!

2	Boxes frozen cheese blintzes	¼	Cup Sugar
½	Cup butter – melted	1	Tbs. vanilla
4	Eggs – beaten	2	Tbs. orange juice concentrate
1 ½	Cup Sour cream	8	Oz. frozen sweetened strawberries

Place frozen blintzes in a casserole baking dish that has been sprayed. Melt butter and slowly add to 4 beaten eggs. Combine the butter and eggs with the sour cream, sugar, vanilla, and orange juice concentrate. Mix well and pour over frozen blintzes.

Bake at 350 for 45 minutes. Serve with frozen sweetened strawberries.

Candied Bacon

* * * * *

And Miss Piggy thought she had all the fun!!

½	Lb. sliced commercial bacon (neither thin nor thick sliced)	2	Cup light brown sugar – loosely packed
			Non stick coating spray

Let the bacon warm to room temperature, then cut the pieces in half crosswise. Spread the brown sugar over a piece of wax paper and press the bacon pieces into the sugar to coat both sides heavily.

Lay the bacon with space between slices on the slotted rack of a broiler pan covered with heavy-duty foil that has been sprayed with a non-stick coating spray. Bake at 350 for 30-40 minutes. Keep checking during the final 15 minutes as it can burn.

Remove the bacon and place on aluminum foil to prevent sticking and let cool to room temp. Store covered at room temperature for up to 24 hours. Do not refrigerate. This is a great recipe to make ahead.

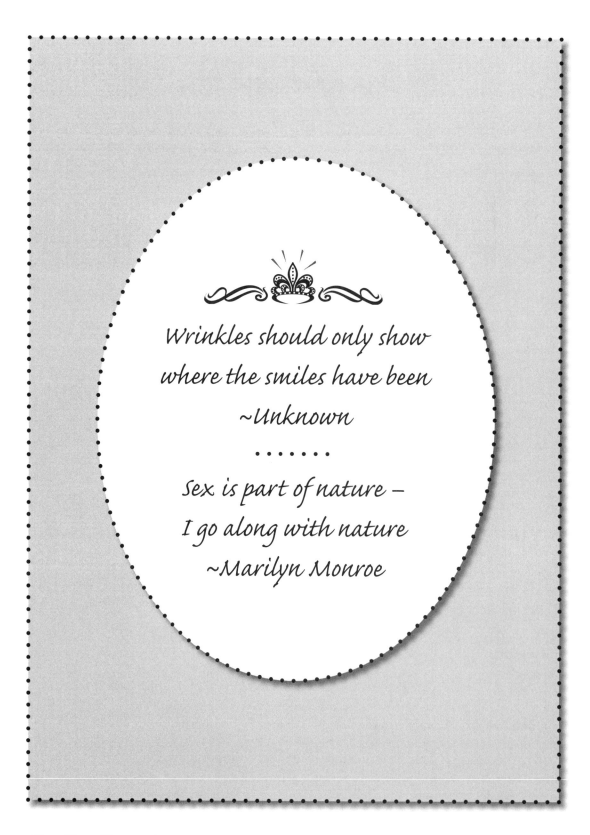

Wrinkles should only show
where the smiles have been
~Unknown

. . . .

Sex is part of nature –
I go along with nature
~Marilyn Monroe

Breakfast Ham Soufflé

* * * * *

*When your Mother-in-law is coming for the weekend and you want
a "tried and true" with "no muss and fuss," this is it.*

5	Eggs	3	Tbs. butter – melted
3	Cups milk	3	Cups French bread – cubed
3	Tbs. flour	2	Cups ham – cubed
1	Tbs. dry mustard	2	4 Oz. cans sliced mushrooms
3	Drops tabasco		

Beat together eggs and milk. Add flour, mustard, Tabasco, butter, bread cubes, ham and mushrooms. Mix together and pour into a prepared 11x7 baking dish. Cover and refrigerate overnight.

Bake uncovered at 350 for 1 hour. May also be placed in soufflé ramekins. Adjust cooking time down to accommodate smaller container.

Apple Sausage Ring

* * * * *

A sensational morning treat!

2	Lb.'s bulk pork sausage	1 ½	Cup seasoned herbed bread crumbs
2	Eggs – lightly beaten		
¼	Cup onion – minced	1	Cup apple – peeled & chopped
½	Cup milk		

Mix all of the above ingredients until thoroughly combined. Form the mixture into a ring on a prepared baking sheet and bake for 60 minutes at 350 or until browned. Drain and cut into serving slices. If using Jimmy Dean brand sausage you may not need to drain. Serve hot.

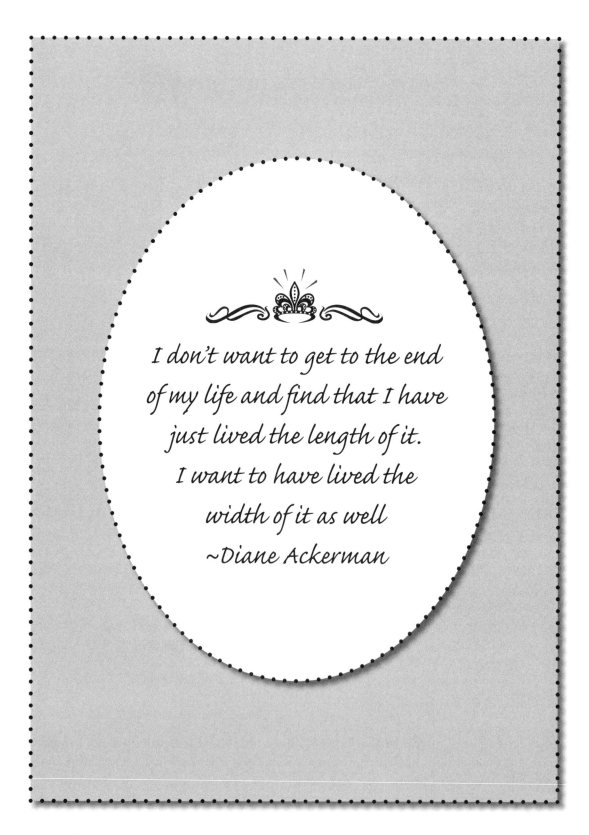

I don't want to get to the end
of my life and find that I have
just lived the length of it.
I want to have lived the
width of it as well
~Diane Ackerman

Oven Baked Sausage & Eggs

* * * * *

*Serve this to your spicy honey on a Sunday morning
and he'll be begging for more!*

1 Lb.	Sweet or hot Italian sausage
½ Lb.	Sharp cheese – grated
½ Tsp.	Dry mustard
½ Tsp.	Paprika
1 Tsp.	Salt
1 C	Sour cream
10-12	Eggs

Skin and crumble sausage in large skillet. Sauté until well done but not overly browned. Drain on paper towels.

Spray 9x12 baking dish with nonstick coating spray. Place half of the cheese on the bottom of dish. In medium bowl, blend mustard, paprika, salt and sour cream; stir in cooked sausage. Spread over grated cheese. (This much can be done the night before and refrigerated.)

When you are ready to bake, beat eggs with a wire whisk in a medium bowl and pour over sausage mixture. Sprinkle remaining half of cheese over top. Bake at 325 for 45 to 60 minutes or until eggs are cooked through and set.

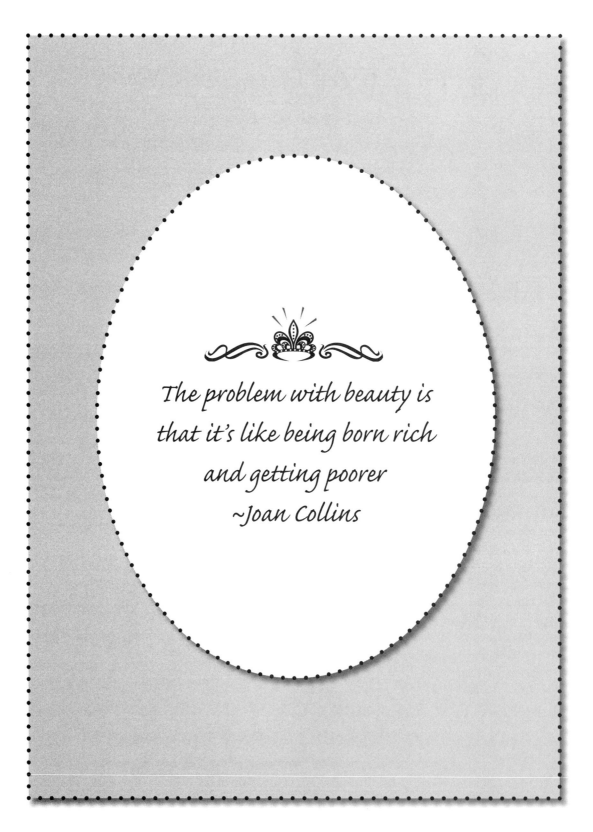

The problem with beauty is that it's like being born rich and getting poorer
~Joan Collins

Cinnamon Coffee Cake

* * * * *

*I could dearly roll myself in butter, sugar, sour cream
and vanilla. Just top me with a cherry!*

1 C	Butter
2 ¾ C	Sugar – divided
2 Tsp.	Vanilla
4	Eggs
3 C	Flour
2 Tsp.	Baking powder
1 Tsp.	Baking soda
1 Tsp.	Salt
2 C	Sour cream
2 Tbs.	Cinnamon
½ C	Walnuts – chopped

In large bowl, cream butter and 2 C sugar until fluffy. Add vanilla. Add eggs, beating after each addition. In a separate mixing bowl, combine flour, baking powder, soda and salt. Slowly add the flour mixture to butter and sugar. Add sour cream and continue to beat until it is completely incorporated. Spoon ⅓ of batter into greased tube pan.

Combine cinnamon, nuts and remaining sugar; sprinkle ⅓ of this over the cake batter. Repeat layers two more times. Bake at 350 for 70 minutes or until done. Cool 10 minutes. Remove from pan.

Depending on your oven, you may need to reduce temperature for last 20 minutes so the top of the cake does not over brown.

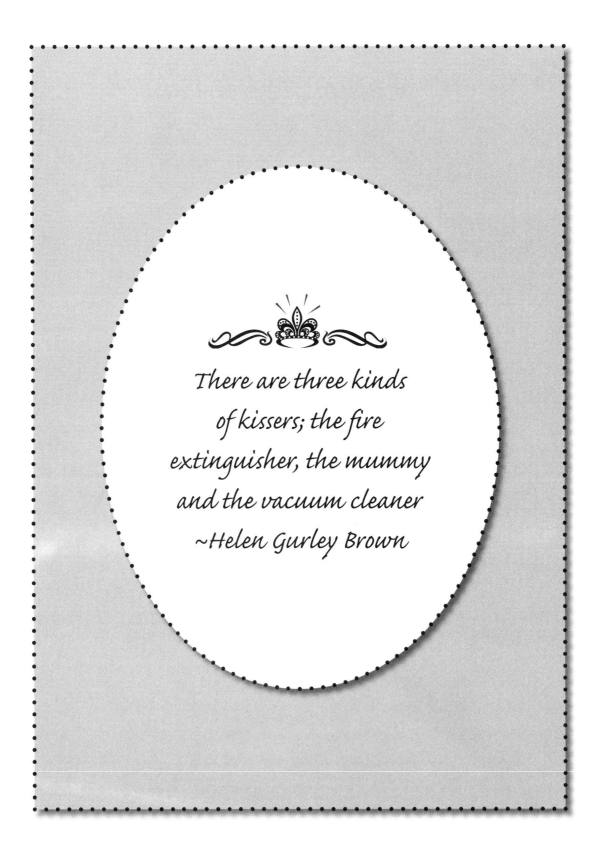

There are three kinds
of kissers; the fire
extinguisher, the mummy
and the vacuum cleaner
~Helen Gurley Brown

Poached Pears with Brandied Cranberries

* * * * *

Simply luscious and divine!

2 C	Cranberry juice
2 Tbs.	Brown sugar
½ Tsp.	Cinnamon
½ Tsp.	Nutmeg
4	Pears – firm, peeled, cored & halved

Brandied Cranberries:

1 ½ Pkg.	Fresh cranberries
1 ½ C	Sugar
¼ C	Brandy

To prepare pears: In a saucepan, bring the cranberry juice, sugar, cinnamon, and nutmeg to a boil. Add the pear halves and simmer for 30 minutes. Refrigerate for 60 minutes or until thoroughly chilled.

Next make the brandied cranberries. Preheat the oven to 350. Lightly grease a 10x15x1 jelly roll pan.

Arrange the cranberries in a single layer on the prepared pan. Top with the sugar. Cover tightly with foil and bake for 45 minutes. Spoon into a bowl and add the brandy, tossing to combine. Chill thoroughly.

Serve the chilled cranberries over the chilled pears.

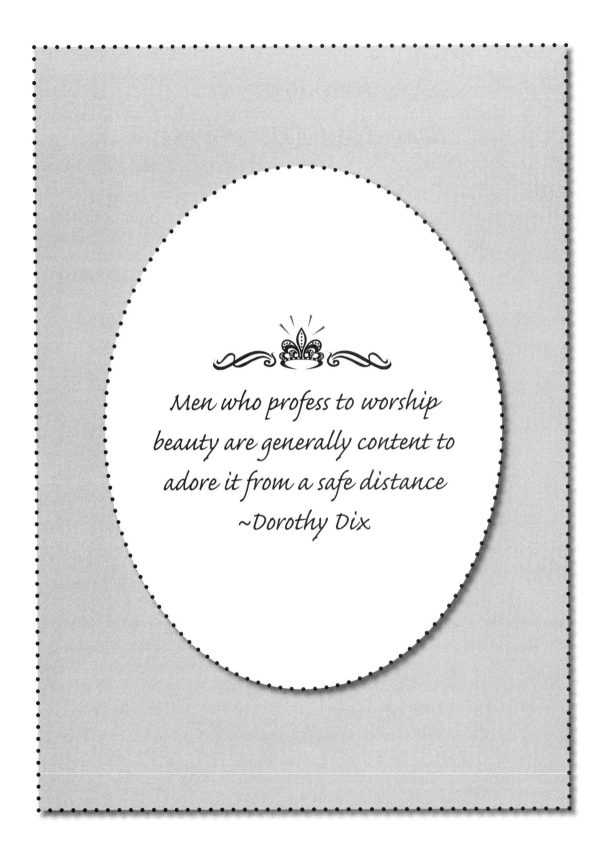

Men who profess to worship beauty are generally content to adore it from a safe distance

~Dorothy Dix

Country Corn Chowder

* * * * *

Emeril's trinity is onion, celery, and green pepper – silly boy,
give me bacon, onion and celery any day!! That and a quart
of cream will send you straight to the promised land.

3 Slices	Bacon – cut in ½-inch pieces
¾ C	Onion – finely chopped
¾ C	Celery – finely chopped
4 C	Chicken stock
4 C	Whole kernel corn – fresh or canned
2 C	Red potatoes – diced
½ Tsp.	Salt
1 C	Heavy cream
2 Tbs.	Fresh parsley – chopped
½ Tsp.	White pepper (if available)
1 Lb.	Chicken breast – poached & cut into 1" cubes

In a large saucepan, fry bacon until crisp. Remove from the pan and pour off all but 2 Tbs. of the drippings. Add the onion and celery and cook until soft and translucent, stirring frequently. In a blender or food processor combine 1 C of the stock and 2 C of the corn, blending until smooth. Add to the sauce pan with the remaining corn, potatoes, stock and salt. Bring to a boil, reduce to simmer, cover and cook for 20 minutes or until potatoes are tender. Whisk in the cream, parsley, and pepper. Add chicken and simmer 3 minutes. Stir in bacon.

Soup is best made a day ahead and reheated slowly to develop flavors.

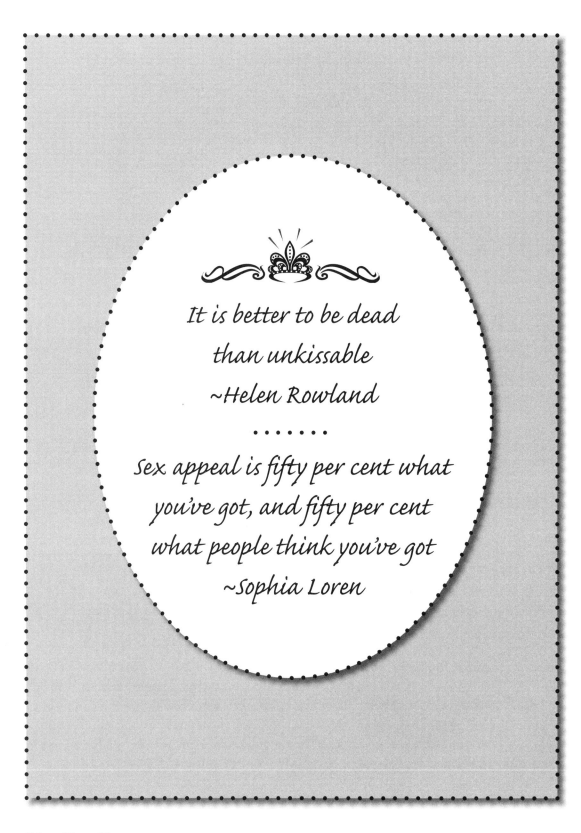

*It is better to be dead
than unkissable
~Helen Rowland*

. . . .

*Sex appeal is fifty per cent what
you've got, and fifty per cent
what people think you've got
~Sophia Loren*

Cream of Wild Rice Soup
* * * * *

*If you want to take this wild one to the next level,
add cream cheese and diced chicken breast – then call me.*

1	Lg. onion – chopped	8	Cup hot turkey broth
½	Green pepper – diced	2	Cup cooked wild rice
1	Stalk celery – diced		Salt & pepper to taste
4-6	Mushrooms, thinly sliced	1	Cup Half & Half
½	Cup butter	1-2	Tbs. dry white wine
1	Cup flour		

Sauté onion, green pepper, celery and mushrooms in butter about 3 minutes or until vegetables are just softened. Sprinkle with flour, stirring and cooking until flour is mixed in and bubbling, but do not brown. Slowly add turkey broth, stirring until well blended. Add wild rice and season to taste with salt and pepper. Heat thoroughly, then stir in cream. Add wine and heat gently, but do not boil.

Tomato-Basil Bisque
* * * * *

*This is a "nooner" staple in our house – quick, pure and simple.
Just add a grilled cheese please.*

2	10 ¾ Oz. tomato soup – undiluted	2 ½	Cup buttermilk
1	14 ½ Oz. Italian style tomatoes – diced	2	Tbs. basil – chopped
		½	Tsp. white pepper
		¼	Tsp. sugar

Blend all ingredients in a saucepan over medium heat, stirring often or until heated through. Garnish with fresh basil and serve immediately.

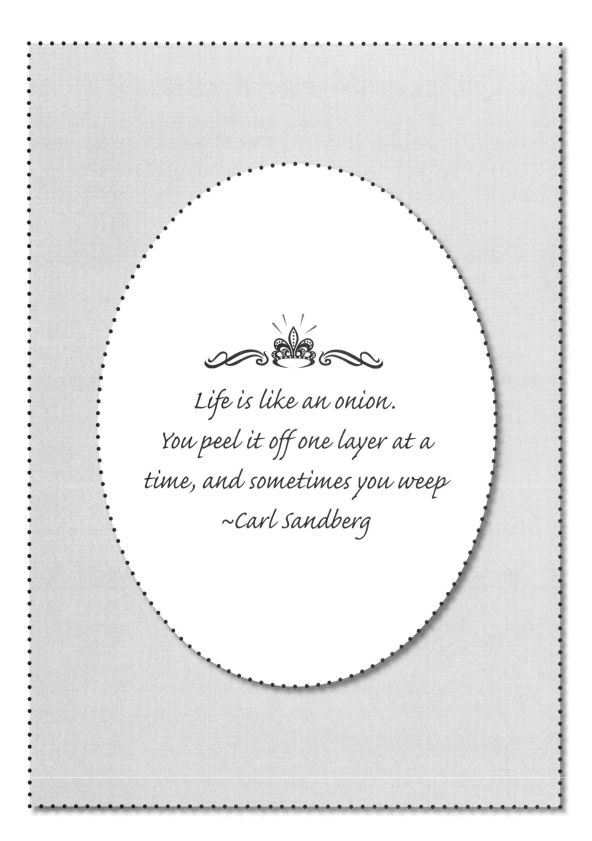

Life is like an onion.
You peel it off one layer at a
time, and sometimes you weep
~Carl Sandberg

French Onion Soup

* * * * *

This is my favorite!! Your husband, lover, and friends will thank you. If you must, do a 50/50 broth (chicken/beef).

½ C	Butter
2 Lb.'s	Sweet onion – thinly sliced
1 Tbs.	Flour
2 Qts.	Chicken stock – canned or fresh
2 C	Dry white wine
	Salt & white pepper to taste
1 Loaf	French bread – sliced
¼ Lb.	Swiss cheese – sliced

Melt ½ of the butter in a saucepan. Cook the onions in it until they are transparent and golden. Add the flour and stir. Cook for three minutes longer. Add the stock and simmer for at least thirty minutes. Add salt and pepper to taste. Toast the bread slices and butter the toast with the remaining butter.

Preheat oven to 375. Pour the soup into a large earthenware casserole. Add the wine and ½ of the grated cheese. Cover the surface with the pieces of buttered toast. Sprinkle all with the remaining grated cheese and add the slices of cheese. The object is to cover the liquid completely with toast and cheese. Place the casserole, uncovered, in the oven for about fifteen minutes, until the cheese and bread are brown and crusty.

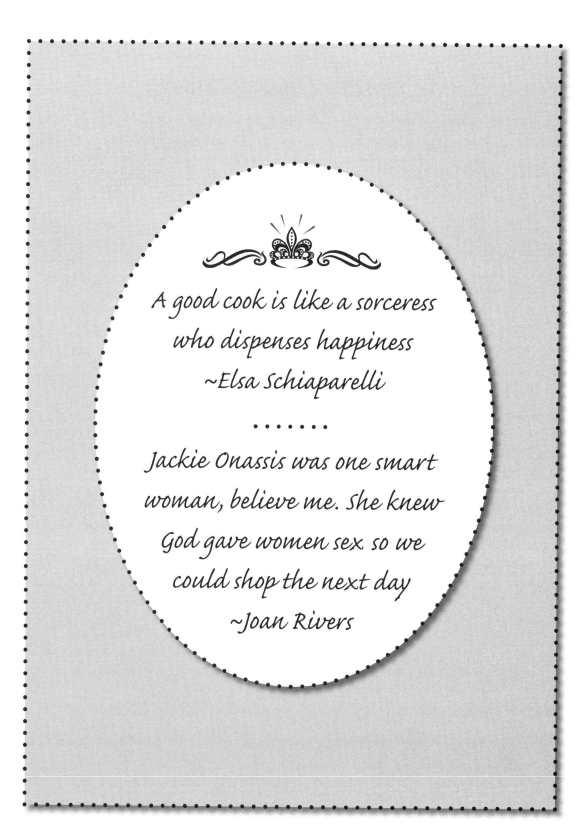

*A good cook is like a sorceress
who dispenses happiness
~Elsa Schiaparelli*

. . . .

*Jackie Onassis was one smart
woman, believe me. She knew
God gave women sex so we
could shop the next day
~Joan Rivers*

Squash & Apple Soup

* * * * *

The acorns are dropping, the pumpkins are frosting,
Eve was tempted with a bite, Adam shouted with joy and
the snake danced in the light of the moon.

½	Cup onion, chopped	¼	Tsp. ground ginger
1	Small carrot, sliced (⅓ cup)	¼	Tsp. white pepper
1¾	Cup apple cider or apple juice	2	Cup cooked mashed acorn
1	Tsp. instant chicken bouillon		squash or one 16 oz. can
	granules		pumpkin
1	Tsp. lemon juice	1	Cup light cream

In a large saucepan cook onion and carrot in apple cider, covered, for 12 minutes. Do not drain. Add bouillon granules, lemon juice, ginger, and pepper. Transfer mixture to a blender or food processor and add squash (or pumpkin) and process until smooth. Transfer back to saucepan, add cream and heat to a boil, stirring constantly. Reduce heat. Cover and simmer 5-10 minutes. To serve, top with sour cream and chives.

Peanut Butter Soup

* * * * *

Who said: "It is better to have loved and lost, than to have never loved
at all"? Who cares when there is a jar of peanut butter in your midst.

½	Cup onions – diced	2 ½	Cup water
½	Cup celery – diced	6	Cup whole milk
¼	Cup bell pepper – diced	1	Cup creamy peanut butter
1	Tsp. garlic – minced	2	Tbs. tomato paste
3	Tbs. butter	3	Tbs. soy sauce
3	Tbs. flour		Chopped peanuts to garnish

In a stock pot sauté the onions, celery, green pepper, and garlic in the butter until soft. Add the flour and cook for 2-3 minutes. Stir in the water and milk, and bring to a boil. Add the peanut butter, tomato paste, and soy sauce. Simmer for 15 minutes. Serve garnished with chopped peanuts.

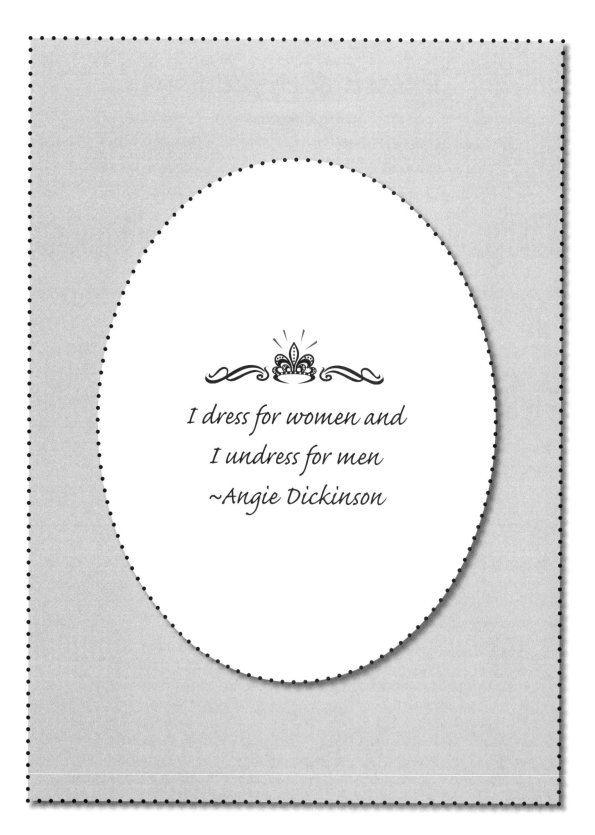

I dress for women and
I undress for men
~Angie Dickinson

Black Bean Soup

* * * * *

Hot Havana nights with steamy Latin dancing –
flavors mixed with music, a memorable evening!

1 Lb.	Black beans
3 Tbs.	Olive oil
1 Med.	Ripe tomato
1	Bay leaf
¼ Med.	Onion
½ Med.	Green pepper
1	Clove garlic – minced
1 Tsp.	Ground oregano
½ Tsp.	Cumin
2 Tbs.	Red wine vinegar
2 Tsp.	Salt
1 Tsp.	Hot pepper sauce
2 Tbs.	Dry Sherry
	Cooked long-grain rice & chopped onions for serving

Wash beans in colander and discard any foreign matter. Place in deep bowl and cover with water. Soak overnight. Pour beans with soaking liquid into 4-quart saucepan. If necessary, add water to cover 1 inch above beans. Add 1 Tbs. olive oil, whole tomato, bay leaf, un-chopped ½ onion and ½ green pepper, and crushed garlic clove. Bring to boil, then simmer, covered, until beans are just tender but not mush, (about 1 hour), stirring occasionally. Discard bay leaf, remaining pieces of tomato, onion, pepper and garlic.

Heat remaining 2 Tbs. olive oil in medium skillet over medium heat. When hot, add remaining finely chopped onion and green pepper. Cook until tender. Add minced garlic, oregano, cumin, vinegar and salt. Stir to combine. Simmer 2 minutes. Add mixture to beans. Stir in hot pepper sauce. Cook, covered 30 minutes. Adjust seasonings to taste. Add Sherry.

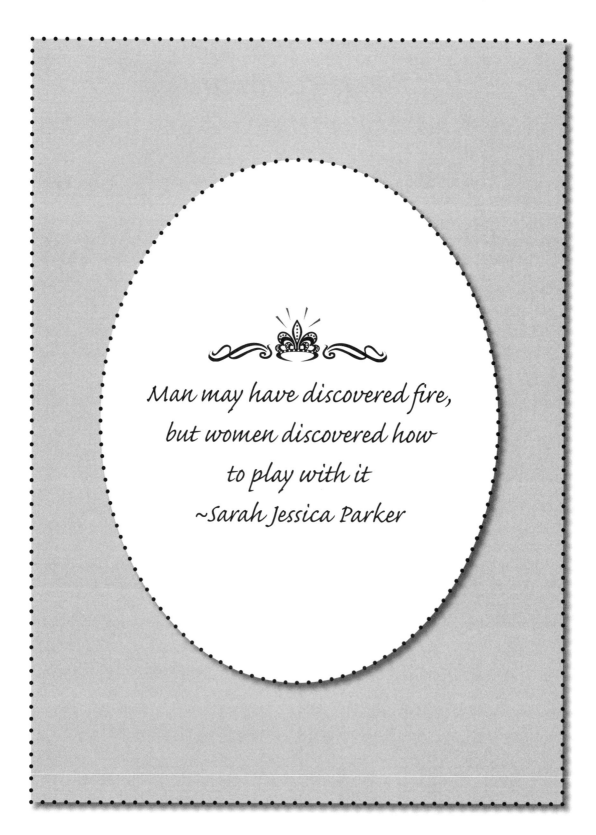

Man may have discovered fire,
but women discovered how
to play with it
~Sarah Jessica Parker

Tortilla Soup

* * * * *

I would have gladly done the Mexican hat dance in my birthday suit to get Chef Christophe's recipe. He was a smart man!

1 Tbs.	Butter
½	Onion – chopped
2 Lg.	Carrots – chopped
½ Med.	Cabbage – chopped
4	Green peppers – chopped
2	Cloves garlic – chopped
	Paprika, oregano, chili powder, cumin – to taste
1 Qt.	Chicken stock
3 Tbs.	Tomato paste
6	6" corn tortillas
8 Oz.	Cheddar cheese (sprinkled)
	Chopped cilantro, diced avocado, salsa, sour cream

Sauté all vegetables with butter until they are soft and tender. Add the spices, stock and continue to cook until all of the flavors have melded. Add tortillas and continue to simmer.

Blend in a food processor in small batches until smooth and creamy. Garnish with cheese, cilantro, avocado, salsa, sour cream, and fried tortilla strips.

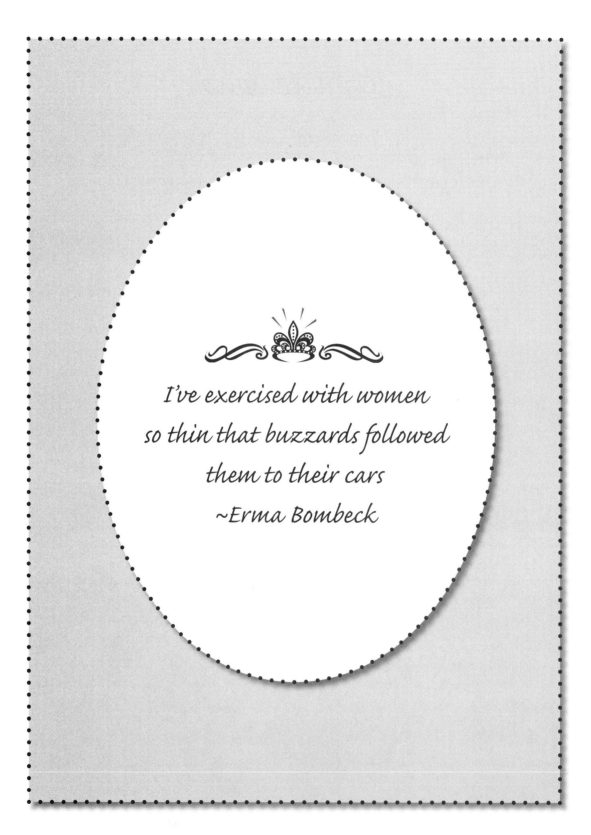

I've exercised with women
so thin that buzzards followed
them to their cars
~Erma Bombeck

Sausage Broccoli Chowder

* * * * *

My hubby gave me the supreme compliment:
"The best I've ever had!" And I thought
he was talking about me!

1 Lb.	Bulk Italian sausage
1 Med.	Onion – chopped
3	Garlic cloves – chopped
8 Oz.	Fresh mushrooms – sliced
2 Tbs.	Butter
2 C	Broccoli florets – frozen is just fine
2-3	Carrots – diced
2 Cans	Chicken broth
1 Can	Condensed cream of mushroom soup – undiluted
9 Oz.	Cheese tortellini – cooked & drained
½ Tsp.	Pepper
1 Tsp.	Italian Seasonings – or more to taste
1 Qt.	Cream
1 Qt.	Light cream
½ C	Parmesan cheese – shredded

In a skillet, cook the crumbled sausage until it is no longer pink but not overly browned. Drain on paper towels and set aside. In the same skillet, sauté onion, garlic and mushrooms in butter until tender. In large saucepan cook the broccoli and carrots in chicken broth until tender. Stir in sausage and the mushroom mixture. Add mushroom soup, tortellini, pepper and seasonings. Stir in creams and parmesan cheese; heat through.

The wife who drives from the back seat isn't any worse than the husband who cooks from the dining-room table
~Unknown

Sweet Potato & Pear Bisque

* * * * *

Mmmmmmm, juicy pears dripping in sugar mixed with the wholesome goodness of sweet potatoes. A match of wonder with just a hint of spice. A Tearoom tradition.

4 C	Chicken broth
¼ C	Onion – ground
½ Tsp.	Pepper
¼ Tsp.	Thyme – ground
1 -40 Oz.	Sweet potatoes
2 -15 Oz.	Canned pears
1-2 Tbs.	Cornstarch
¼ -½ C	Heavy cream

Bring chicken broth to boil with onion, thyme and pepper. Process undrained sweet potatoes and pears in a food processor until smooth. You may need to do this in batches depending upon the capacity of your processor. Add a couple of tablespoons of cornstarch to last processing batch. Add pear and sweet potato mixture to gently boiling broth. Continue to cook until cornstarch has glazed the back of your spoon and cooked through.

Make the day ahead so flavors can meld. When re-heating add enough cream to blend. Do not boil as the soup will curdle!!! Season with salt to taste and adjust pepper and thyme to liking.

I like to buy clothes that are two sizes too small and then take them in a little
~Dolly Parton

Cran-Apple-Berry Soup

* * * * *

*I have a secret: SHHHHHHH – don't tell – you can use
a tablespoon or two of Aspen Mulling Spices in place of
cinnamon and cloves.*

1 Qt.	Apple cider
1 Pkg.	Fresh or frozen cranberries
1 Lb.	Frozen whole strawberries
¾ C	Brown sugar
¾ C	Sugar
1 Tbs.	Lemon juice
1 Tsp.	Cinnamon
¼ Tsp.	Cloves
1-2 Tbs.	Cornstarch
	Heavy cream

Bring cider, cranberries and strawberries to boil in large saucepan. Add sugars, lemon juice, cinnamon, and cloves. Simmer for 10-15 minutes until cranberries have popped and released their juice. Remove from heat and let cool. Fruit will rise to the top. Skim fruit off. Strain remaining liquid. Add enough liquid to cornstarch to blend and return to saucepan with balance of soup mix. Heat to boil to thicken slightly. Remove and chill until ready to serve.

When ready to serve add enough cream to the soup base to bring to a deep mauve color. Tasting will help you. This may be served either warm or chilled. Top with a dollop of whipping cream. Note: Depending on how sweet or tart you like your soup, you may need to adjust sugar and add more to sweeten.

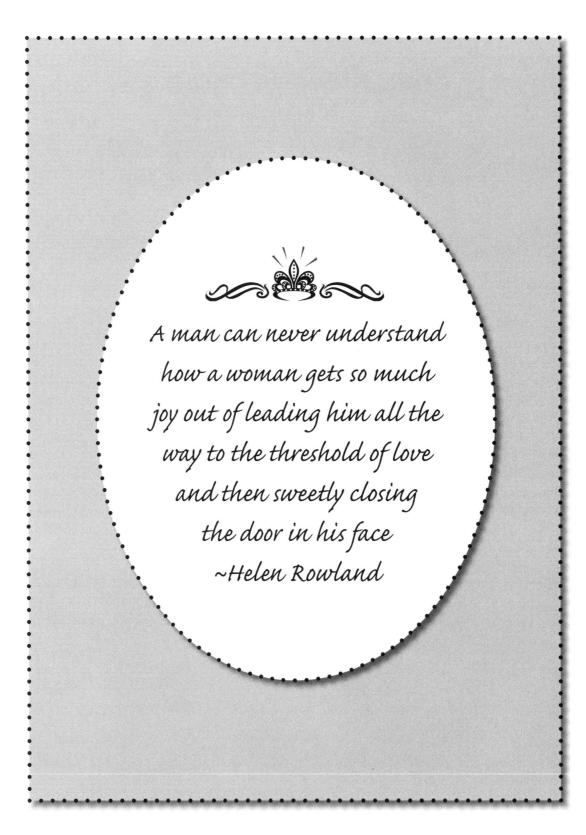

*A man can never understand
how a woman gets so much
joy out of leading him all the
way to the threshold of love
and then sweetly closing
the door in his face
~Helen Rowland*

Dill Pickle Soup

* * * * *

This is the sexiest and most sensual soup I've ever made!!!
If you buy this cookbook for one reason and one reason only,
it will be for this recipe.

3 Tbs.	Butter
½ C	Onion – chopped
½ C	White wine
⅓ C + 1 Tbs.	Flour
5 C	Water
1 ½ C	Marinade from dill pickles
4	Large dill pickles – chopped
2 Tsp.	Dried dill weed
	Whipping cream
	Poultry seasoning
	Salt & white pepper

Melt the butter in large saucepan over medium heat. Add onion and sauté until soft. Add wine and continue cooking until liquid almost evaporates. Reduce the heat and stir in flour. Be sure not to brown!!. Add water and pickle juice. Heat to boil while stirring and soup begins to thicken. Add pickles and dill weed. Remove from heat and let cool slightly. In the food processor puree in small batches. After each batch, strain into a saucepan until all the stock is finished. Add cream, poultry seasoning, salt and pepper to taste. Divine!!!!

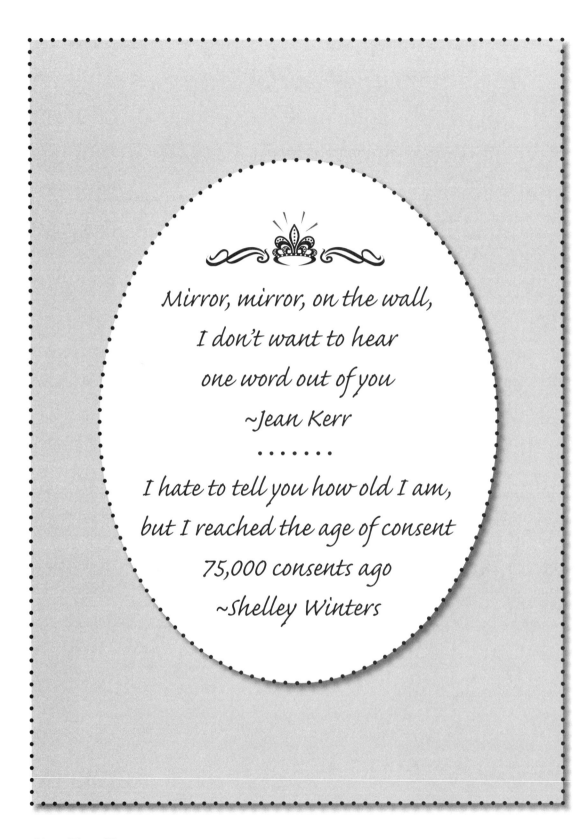

Mirror, mirror, on the wall,
I don't want to hear
one word out of you
~Jean Kerr

• • • • • • •

I hate to tell you how old I am,
but I reached the age of consent
75,000 consents ago
~Shelley Winters

Fruit Curry Soup

* * * * *

*Spice is so nice. Just a little to start if you're timid or shy —
you can always kick it up a tidge.*

1 ½	Tbs. curry powder	1	Watermelon – slice
2	Tbs. flour	4	Apricots
3	Tbs. butter	4	Peaches
4	Cups chicken stock	½	Tsp. salt
4	Plums	6	Tbs. lemon juice
¼	Cantaloupe	1	Cup Half & Half

Bring the curry powder, flour, butter and stock to a boil and cook for about ten minutes, until the mixture thickens. Cool. Remove the rinds and pits from the fruits and puree them through a sieve or in an electric blender. Add the puree to the cooled soup stock. Stir well. Add the salt and lemon juice and mix in the cream. Chill.

Italian Sausage & Potato Soup

* * * * *

*When Chef Judd came up with this winner, the Tearoom
had just opened – the ladies were wowed!! As always,
the key is a good long hot Italian sausage.*

1	Onion – chopped	4	Cups chicken stock
3	Stalks celery – diced	4	Potatoes – large russets peeled & chopped
3	Tbs. butter		
½	Lb. hot Italian sausage – Graziano's, if available	2	Cups cream
			Salt & pepper to taste

In large pot, sauté onion and celery in butter until translucent and soft. Add sausage and brown. Drain fat and return to stock pot. Add chicken stock and potatoes. Simmer until potatoes are tender. When ready, add cream and salt to taste.

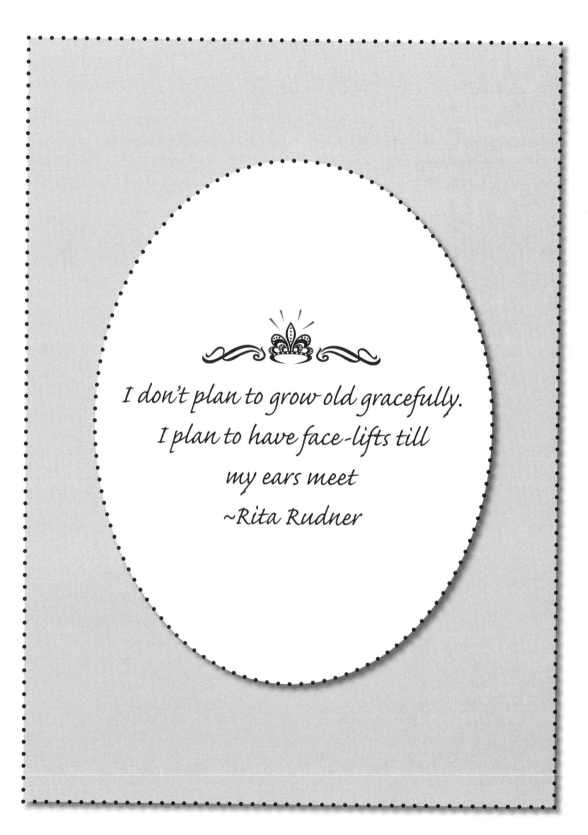

I don't plan to grow old gracefully.
I plan to have face-lifts till
my ears meet
~Rita Rudner

Pumpkin Bisque with Fresh Sage

* * * * *

Have you ever thought of jumping in a vat with something so good you would die for it? I have – this is a pairing made in heaven.

3 Tbs.	Butter
1 ½ C	Leeks – chopped (white & pale green parts only)
1 ½ C	Carrot – peeled & chopped
½ C	Yellow onion – chopped
4	Garlic cloves – peeled & chopped
½ Tsp.	Dried thyme – crumbled
1	Bay leaf
6 ½ C	Chicken stock
1 Lg. Can	Pumpkin – solid pack
2 Tbs.	Dark brown sugar
	Freshly ground black pepper – to taste
¼ Tsp.	Nutmeg – freshly grated
⅓ C	Whipping cream
2 Tbs.	Sage leaves – minced

In a large heavy pot melt the butter. Add the leek, carrot, onion, garlic, thyme and bay leaf. Cover and cook, stirring once or twice, for 10 minutes. Add the chicken stock, pumpkin, brown sugar, 1 Tsp. salt, ½ Tsp. pepper and the nutmeg. Bring to a simmer, then partially cover, lower the heat and cook, stirring occasionally for 30 minutes. Remove from the heat. Cool slightly, then puree the soup in batches in a food processor. Cool completely then cover and refrigerate.

May be made up to 3 days ahead. When ready to serve, bring the soup to a simmer in a large pot. Stir in the cream and the sage. Adjust the seasoning. Simmer, stirring often for 5 minutes. Serve hot.

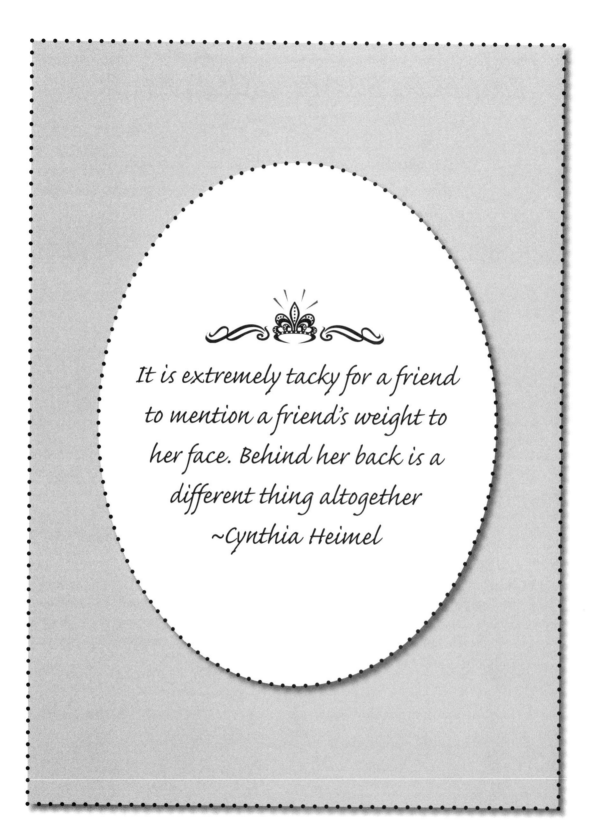

It is extremely tacky for a friend to mention a friend's weight to her face. Behind her back is a different thing altogether
~Cynthia Heimel

Lentil Stew

* * * * *

*sherry will add a depth of flavor – remember just a splash –
then one or two for the cook.*

5 C	Chicken or vegetable stock
1 C	Lentils – rinsed
½ Tsp.	Thyme
½ Tsp.	Marjoram
1	Bay leaf – crushed
2-4 Tbs.	Olive oil
2	Onions – chopped
4	Carrots – diced
1 -15 Oz.	Tomatoes – whole, cut up
¼ C	Dry sherry
	Salt & pepper – to taste
¼ C	Parsley – chopped
	Grated Swiss, Monterey Jack or Cheddar cheese

In a large stock pot bring the stock, lentils, and seasonings to boil. Cover and simmer 20-30 minutes, or until the lentils are tender. Meanwhile, heat the olive oil and sauté the onions and carrots. Cover and simmer until the carrots are crispy-tender. Stir the carrots and onions into the lentil mixture, along with the tomatoes, sherry, salt, and pepper. Simmer for 1 hour. Stir in the parsley.

Place the cheese in the bottom of each bowl and fill with stew.

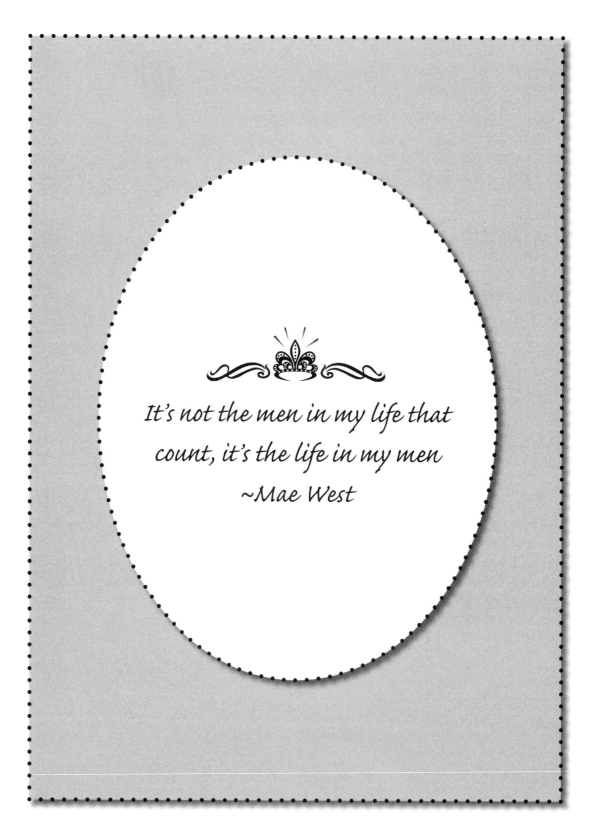

It's not the men in my life that count, it's the life in my men
~Mae West

Apple-Walnut with Cranberry Vinaigrette

* * * * *

Your eyes meet across a crowded room, your throat takes a little lunge and your heart skips a beat. Then suddenly you realize the exotic flavors of the cranberries, apples and walnuts lingering on your tongue; these are the most important flavors of the moment! Not!!!!

¼ C	Fresh or frozen cranberries – thawed
¼ C	Balsamic vinegar
1 Tbs.	Red onion – chopped
1 Tbs.	Sugar
1 Tsp.	Dijon mustard
1 C.	Vegetable oil
10 C	Mixed Baby Greens
2	Red Delicious apples – cored & thinly sliced
½ C	Walnuts – toasted & chopped

Puree cranberries in processor until smooth. Add vinegar, onion, sugar and mustard. Process until well blended. With processor running, gradually add oil and process until blended. Transfer to bowl. Season to taste with salt and pepper. Combine greens and apples in large bowl. Toss with enough dressing to coat. Sprinkle with walnuts.

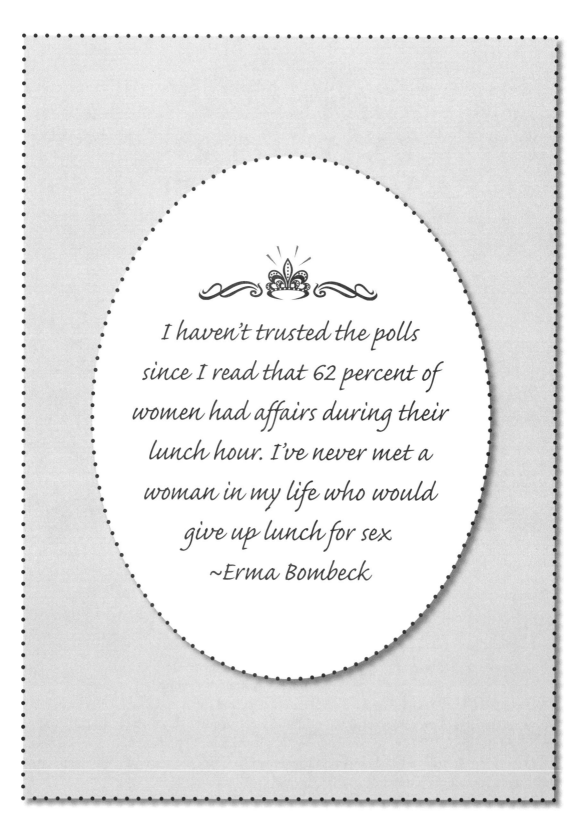

*I haven't trusted the polls
since I read that 62 percent of
women had affairs during their
lunch hour. I've never met a
woman in my life who would
give up lunch for sex
~Erma Bombeck*

Spinach Salad
* * * * *

Love & marriage, love & marriage, go together like a horse
and carriage. This will bring a song to your heart.

½	Cup vegetable oil	2	10 Oz. baby spinach
¼	Cup ketchup	1	Cup cherry tomatoes – halved
¼	Cup red wine vinegar	2	8 Oz. water chestnuts –
¼	Cup onion – finely chopped		drained & sliced
3	Tbs. sugar	2	Cups chow mein noodles
2	Tsp. Worcestershire sauce	2	Eggs – hard cooked & chopped
½	Tsp. salt	12	Bacon slices – cooked & crumbled

In a food processor or blender, add the oil, ketchup, red wine vinegar, onion, sugar, Worcestershire sauce and salt. Blend until completely incorporated. Chill until ready to serve.

In your favorite salad bowl combine the spinach, cherry tomatoes, water chestnuts, Chow mein noodles, eggs and bacon. Pour chilled dressing over salad and toss until completed mixed.

Frozen Banana Salad
* * * * *

The kids will have fun chasing this all over the plate – it'll keep them
entertained while you're busy doing those other things!!

2	3 Oz. cream cheese – softened	½	Cup pineapple –
½ -1	Tsp. salt		crushed & drained
½	Cup mayonnaise	2	Medium bananas – sliced
1	Lemon – juiced	½	Cup walnuts – chopped
		1	Cup heavy cream – whipped

Combine cream cheese, salt, mayonnaise and lemon juice in your mixer and cream until smooth. Add the drained pineapple, sliced bananas and chopped walnuts to the cream cheese mixture. Fold in cream, mixing thoroughly. Freeze salad until firm. Allow salad to thaw for about 1 hour before serving.

I got my figure back after giving birth. Sad, I'd hoped to get somebody else's

~Caroline Quentin

Winter Salad

* * * * *

I could sing: Winter, Spring, Summer or Fall,
all you have to do is just call – Just promise him you'll be there.

Dressing:

¾ C	Olive oil
3 Tbs.	Lemon juice
3 Tbs.	Sherry wine vinegar
1 Tbs.	Dijon mustard
⅛ Tsp.	Salt & pepper – each

Salad:

8 C	Mixed Greens
1 Med.	Red onion – sliced
2	Crisp apples, Fuji, Braeburn or York – thinly sliced
½ C	Pecan halves – toasted
½ C	Crumbled bleu cheese
½ C	Dried cranberries

In a small mixing bowl add lemon juice, sherry wine vinegar and Dijon mustard. Whisk until mixed. Add salt & pepper. Slowly add olive oil while whisking to incorporate and emulsify the dressing. Chill.

In your favorite salad bowl, add the washed and ready mixed greens. Top with the red onion, chopped apples, toasted pecan halves, crumbled bleu cheese and dried cranberries. Chill.

When ready to serve, shake the chilled dressing and pour over the salad.

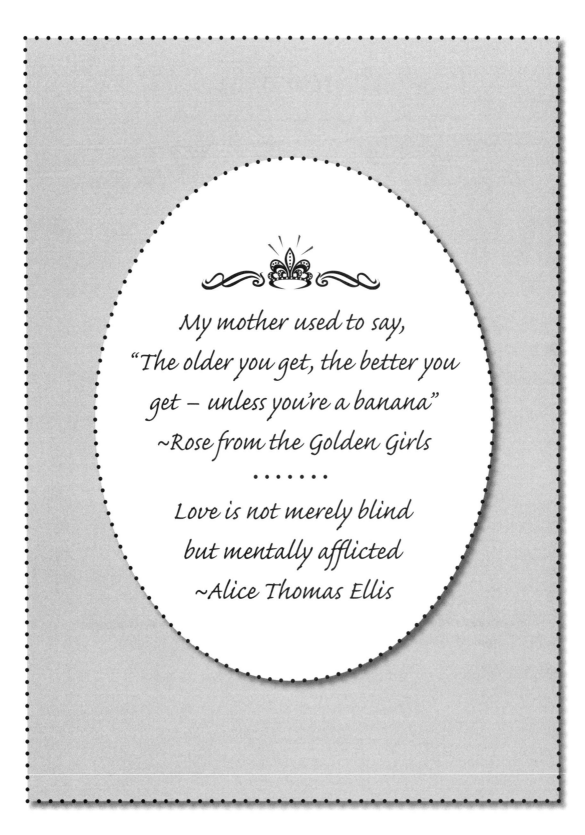

My mother used to say,
"The older you get, the better you
get – unless you're a banana"
~Rose from the Golden Girls

. . . .

Love is not merely blind
but mentally afflicted
~Alice Thomas Ellis

Fruit Salad
* * * * *

My produce manager is my best friend. He and I love to chat
while squeezing all kinds of luscious fruits and crisp vegetables.
He knows what's good, what's fresh and all my secrets.
I'd take him home to meet my mother any day.

2	Golden Delicious apples – diced	2	16 Oz. Mandarin oranges – drained
2	Red Delicious apples – diced		Green grapes
4	Bananas, sliced		Red grapes
2	20 Oz. pineapple chunks – drained		Fresh sliced peaches (in season, opt.)
			Vanilla yogurt

In a large bowl combine all diced and sliced fruits. Toss with yogurt chill. Serve.

Note: In place of vanilla yogurt, you may try Pear Yogurt. It's delicious.

Fabulous Cranberry Salad
* * * * *

My mother had a whole kitchen drawer devoted to Jell-O. She was dubbed
the Jell-O Queen in our house! And, Dad never said a word.

1	8 Oz. crushed pineapple	1	8 Oz. cream cheese
2	Cups liquid	1	Cup whipping cream – whipped
2	3 Oz. raspberry or cherry Jell-O	1	16 Oz. can whole cranberry sauce
2	Tbs. salad dressing (Miracle Whip)	½	Cup walnuts – chopped
		½	Cup apple (Gala) – diced

Drain juice from fruit. Add water to make 2 Cups liquid. Heat and dissolve Jell-O in hot liquid. Mash cream cheese with salad dressing. Beat into liquid. Add whipped cream. Fold in remaining ingredients. Chill until set and ready to serve.

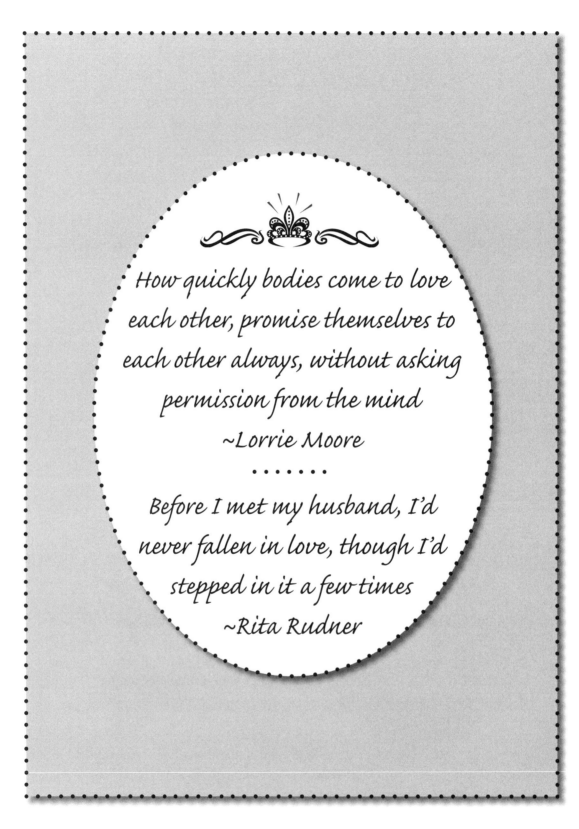

How quickly bodies come to love each other, promise themselves to each other always, without asking permission from the mind
~Lorrie Moore

. . . .

Before I met my husband, I'd never fallen in love, though I'd stepped in it a few times
~Rita Rudner

Spring Spinach Salad

* * * * *

You will adore the newness of a tender leaf and the delicate sweetness
of a ripe strawberry mixed with the textures of tart and savory.
Just like two lips waiting to meet for their first event.

10	Cups baby spinach	½	Cup crumbled bleu cheese
2	Cups strawberries – fresh	4-6	Bacon slices – cooked & crumbled
1	Cup pecans – toasted		Briana's Poppyseed Dressing

In your prettiest salad bowl, place baby spinach, quartered strawberries, toasted pecans and crumbled blue cheese. In a small skillet sauté bacon until crisp but not burned. Drain and crumble. Add cooled bacon to salad mix.

Toss with Briana's Poppyseed Dressing that has been chilled. Serve immediately.

Note: I have made my own poppyseed dressing from every available recipe and I don't believe any compares with the flavor or texture of Briana's. I find the homemade dressing to be thick and unmanageable.

Seafood Pasta Salad

* * * * *

Don't you just love seafood? Any excuse to talk to a man in the grocery store.

1	Lb. small shell pasta noodles		Hot pepper sauce to taste –
1 ½	Cups mayonnaise		if desired
¾	Cup chili sauce	1	Lb. imitation crab meat – chopped
1	Tbs. parsley – chopped	¼	Lb. cooked shrimp – chopped
1 ½	Tsp. lemon juice	4	Stalks celery – chopped
2	Tsp. horseradish	1	Onion – chopped
	Salt & pepper		Seafood seasoning to taste

Cook pasta according to package directions. Cool and place in large bowl. Add crab meat, shrimp, celery and onion to pasta. In a separate mixing bowl combine mayonnaise, chili sauce, parsley, lemon juice, horseradish, salt, pepper, and hot sauce. After blending, add to pasta and seafood mixture. Refrigerate and allow flavors to blend. Sprinkle with seafood seasoning. If needed, add salt, pepper, and additional seafood seasonings.

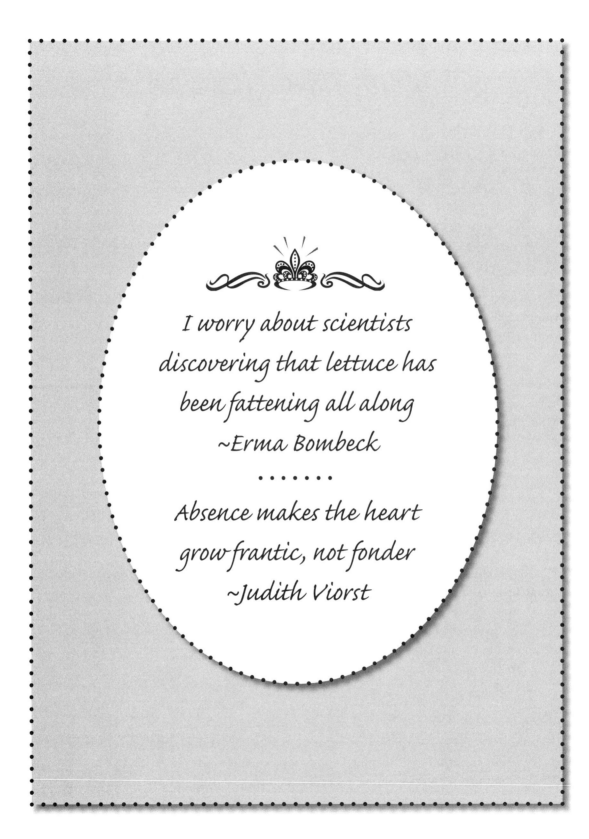

I worry about scientists
discovering that lettuce has
been fattening all along
~Erma Bombeck

Absence makes the heart
grow frantic, not fonder
~Judith Viorst

Green Salad

* * * * *

*People who love food and enjoy cooking will forever hold
a place in my heart. "Like minds," I guess –*

	Iceberg lettuce – torn	1	Jar 3-Bean Salad (prepared brand like S&W) – drained
	Red Leaf lettuce – torn	1	Can hearts of palm – drained & chunked
	Cherry tomatoes – halved	1	Jar black olives – drained (optional)
1	Jar pickled beets – drained		Croutons – optional
1	Can baby corn – drained		Girards Original Salad dressing
1	Jar marinated artichoke hearts – drained		

This recipe will take a very large salad bowl. Tear lettuces and add all remaining ingredients with the exception of the salad dressing. Keep chilled until the salad is ready to serve. Top with the dressing and enjoy.

Chinese Chicken Salad

* * * * *

*If you're looking for a "quickie," this fits the bill. I always keep a
can of tuna or chicken breast meat in my pantry for a last minute fix-it.*

1	Bag Greener Selection Greens	½	Cup dry roasted peanuts
1	Can water chestnuts – sliced & drained	3-4	Green onions chopped (whites and some green)
1	Can Mandarin oranges – drained		Chinese noodles
1	Large can chicken breast meat		Girards Oriental Salad Dressing

In a large salad bowl combine the first 6 well chilled ingredients and toss with chilled salad dressing. Top with Chinese noodles and serve immediately.

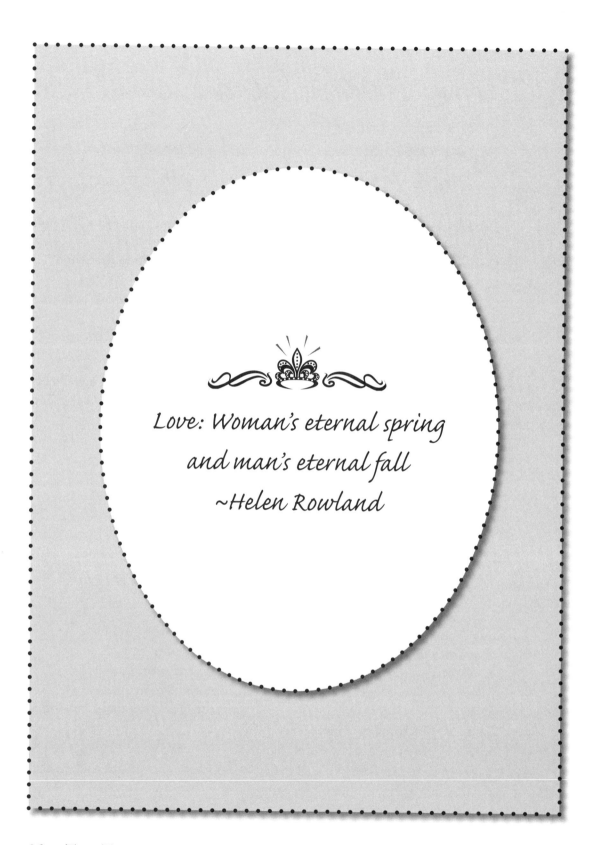

Love: Woman's eternal spring
and man's eternal fall
~Helen Rowland

New Year's Eve Apple Salad

* * * * *

*No reason to go out for New Years when you have this recipe
at your fingertips. That certain question might get popped
on a night like this!*

10 C	Mixed greens
2	Granny Smith apples – chopped
6-8	Bacon slices – cooked & crumbled
	Sliced almonds

In a skillet, sauté bacon slices until done but not burned. Remove and drain on a paper towel. When cool, crumble and set aside

In a small non stick skillet heat 2 Tbs. of butter (not margarine) and add sliced (not slivered) almonds. Gently brown almonds while stirring constantly over medium heat being careful not to burn.

Freshen mixed greens and combine with chopped apples, crumbled bacon. Toss with dressing. Top with toasted buttered almonds and serve immediately.

Dressing:

½ C	Oil – Canola
6 Tbs.	Tarragon wine vinegar
1 Tsp.	Dry mustard
2 Tbs.	Sugar
1 Tsp.	Salt
½ Tsp.	Pepper

In a small mixing bowl with lid combine all ingredients. Shake until sugar is dissolved and blended. Chill until ready to serve.

A woman has got to love a
bad man once or twice in her
life to be thankful for a good one
~Marjorie Kinnan Rawlings

. . . .

I'm a loser. When I grew my own
bustle, they went out of style
~Erma Bombeck

Hot Spiced Fruit
* * * * *

This is so yummy. It's a must on your holiday table along with the other trimmings of the season. After me, this is my husband's late night snack. He loves the leftovers on ice cream.

1	29 Oz. pear halves – drained	1	Jar Maraschino cherries – drained
1	29 Oz. pineapple sliced – drained	⅓	Cup butter
1	16 Oz. apricot halves – drained	1	Cup brown sugar – firmly packed
1	11 Oz. Mandarin oranges – drained	1	Tsp. cinnamon
1	29 Oz. peaches – drained	¼	Tsp. cloves
		2	Tsp. curry powder

Drain all fruit and pat dry with paper towels. Arrange in 9x13 buttered glass baking dish. Melt butter in saucepan over low heat. Stir in brown sugar, cinnamon, cloves and curry powder. Remove from heat and spoon over fruit. Bake in 325 degree oven 30 minutes or until bubbly.

Hot German Potato Salad
* * * * *

Great with Polish Kielbasa. You can just polka around the deck with your "honey" while its grilling.

8-10	Potatoes – medium, boiled	½	Cup vinegar
½	Cup onion – diced	¾	Cup sugar
5	Eggs – hard-boiled & sliced	3	Tbs. flour
6-10	Bacon slices – cooked & crumbled	1	Tbs. salt
3-4	Tbs. bacon grease	1	Tsp. celery seed
½	Cup water		Egg & bacon for garnish

Peel and slice the potatoes. In a large serving bowl or dish, layer the onion, sliced eggs, bacon, and potatoes. In a skillet bring the bacon drippings, water, and vinegar to a boil. In a bowl combine the sugar, flour, salt, and celery seed. Pour the hot liquid into the dry ingredients and stir well. Return the mixture to the skillet and bring to a boil, stirring until thickened. Pour over the layered mixture. Garnish with egg and bacon. Serve immediately.

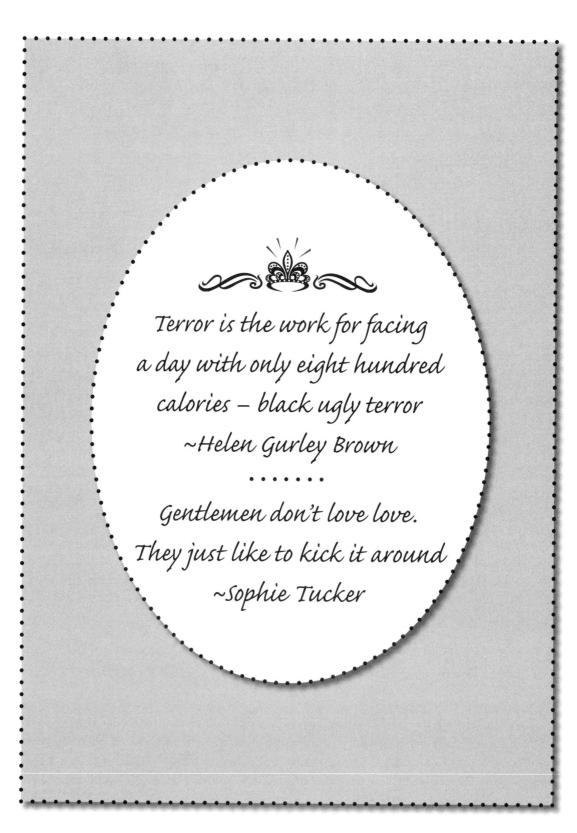

Terror is the work for facing
a day with only eight hundred
calories – black ugly terror
~Helen Gurley Brown

. . . .

Gentlemen don't love love.
They just like to kick it around
~Sophie Tucker

Maple Salad

* * * * *

This recipe alone is worth having the boss over for dinner!!

Dressing:

¼	Cup rice wine vinegar	½	Tsp. dry mustard
½	Cup Canola oil	1	Shallot – minced
½	Cup maple syrup		Salt & pepper – to taste

In a small bowl combine rice wine vinegar, syrup, mustard, shallot, salt and pepper. Add Canola oil and mix all ingredients together. Chill

½	Lb. bacon – fried	½	Bag baby spinach
2	Vidalia onions – thinly sliced	¾	Cup pecan halves
1	Head boston lettuce	¼	Lb. Romano cheese – thinly sliced

In a large skillet, fry bacon till crisp; remove to paper towels to drain, and crumble. Reduce heat to medium and add onions. Caramelize onion slices in bacon fat stirring occasionally.

Assemble lettuce and spinach in a large salad bowl. Top with pecans, bacon, cheese strips and caramelized onion slices. Pour chilled dressing over all. Toss and serve.

Gingery Fruit Slaw

* * * * *

When you're invited to a picnic to meet a certain new someone, take this along to impress!

Salad:

1	Head cabbage – shredded
4	Bartlett pears – peeled & chopped
1 ½	Cups seedless grapes – cut into halves

Dressing:

1	Cup mayonnaise
6	Tbs. lemon juice
3	Tbs. sugar
½	Tsp. grated fresh ginger
1	Tsp. grated lemon rind

Combine shredded cabbage and fruit in large salad bowl. Mix dressing ingredients thoroughly to dissolve sugar. Gradually pour dressing over salad mixture (you may not need all). Toss gently and chill. Drain excess dressing from salad before serving.

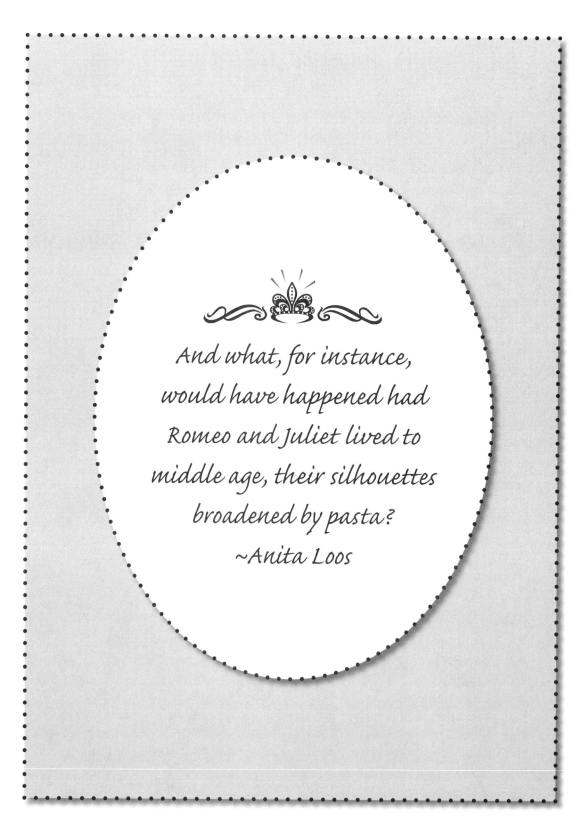

And what, for instance, would have happened had Romeo and Juliet lived to middle age, their silhouettes broadened by pasta?
~Anita Loos

Bow Tie Pasta

* * * * *

I just love a handsome Greek god, brings back
fond memories of my youth – Get my fan!!!

8 Oz.	Bow-tie pasta
½	Green bell pepper – chopped
½	Red bell pepper – chopped
⅓ C	Feta cheese – crumbled
1	Stalk celery chopped
12	Kalamata olives – pitted & chopped
	Salt & pepper – to taste
¼ C	Pasta dressing
	Fresh basil
	Tomato wedges for garnish

In a medium sauce pan, heat salted water to boil and cook bow tie pasta according to package directions. Drain and cool in a salad bowl. Toss pasta with green pepper, red pepper, Feta cheese, chopped celery, Kalamata olives, salt, and pepper. Mix in pasta dressing until dressed. If needed, add more dressing. Cover and chill at least 2 hours before serving. Adjust seasoning, dressing, and top with chopped basil and tomato wedges.

Pasta Salad Dressing:

¼ C	Balsamic vinegar
¼ C	Olive oil
¼ C	Vegetable oil
1 Tbs.	Parsley – chopped
1	Green onion – chopped
1 Tbs.	Garlic – minced
1 Tsp.	Lemon juice
½ Tsp.	Dried basil
½ Tsp.	Dried tarragon
¼ Tsp.	Salt
	Freshly ground pepper

Whisk together all ingredients in a small bowl until blended. Chill until ready to serve.

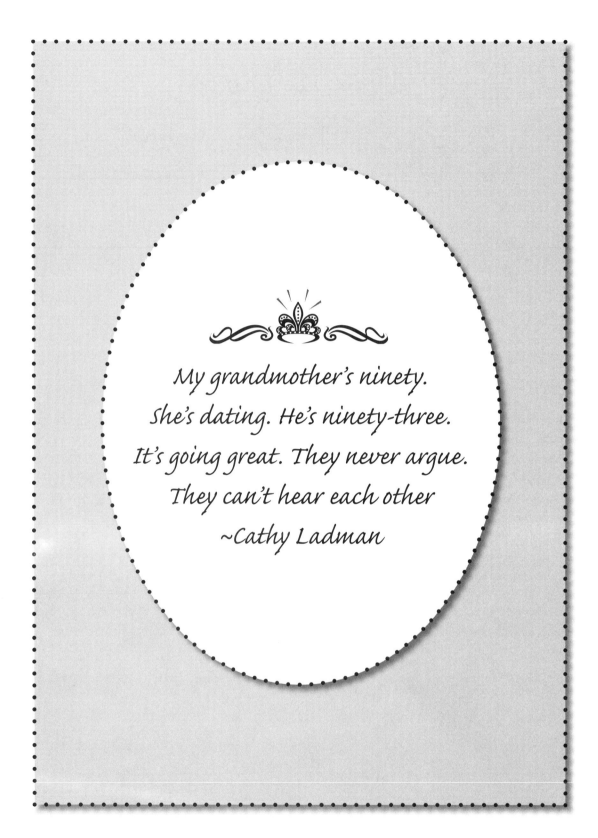

My grandmother's ninety.
She's dating. He's ninety-three.
It's going great. They never argue.
They can't hear each other
~Cathy Ladman

Salad Dressings:

* * * * *

*Let your husband know you like to experiment and
add a little zest to your life. Try one of these.*

Raspberry Vinaigrette

2	Tbs. seedless raspberry jam		2	Tbs. fresh orange juice
2	Shallots – finely chopped		1	Cup olive oil
1	Tbs. Dijon mustard		¼	Cup raspberry vinegar
2	Tbs. balsamic vinegar			Salt & pepper
2	Tbs. honey			

In a medium bowl, combine jam, chopped shallots and mustard with the balsamic and raspberry vinegar. Add honey and orange juice and whisk to blend. Drizzle in the olive oil while continuously whisking until blended. Chill. Keep unused dressing in refrigerator.

Apple Cider Vinaigrette

½	Cup Canola oil		½	Tsp. pepper
¾	Cup apple cider		1	Tsp. Grey Poupon
½	Cup cider vinegar		¼	Tsp. celery seed
2	Tbs. sugar		1	Tsp. grated onion
½	Tsp. salt			

Combine all dressing ingredients in jar with lid. Shake well and chill until ready to serve. Keep unused dressing in refrigerator.

Strawberry Vinaigrette

1	Lb. bag frozen strawberries, thawed		⅔	Cup cider vinegar
1	Cup Canola oil		½	Cup sugar
				Salt – to taste

In food processor blend strawberries until smooth, add vinegar, sugar and salt. Continue to process while slowly adding canola oil. Chill until ready to serve. Refrigerate any unused dressing.

(Dressings continued on next page.)

Please don't retouch my wrinkles.
It took me so long to earn them
~Anna Magnani

Green Goddess Dressing

1 ¾	Cups mayo		1	Tbs. parsley
¼	Cup sour cream		¼	Cup tarragon vinegar
3	Tbs. tarragon leaves		1	Clove garlic – minced
2	Tbs. chives			

Combine ingredients in a jar and shake. Let stand at least one hour in refrigerator for flavors to incorporate. Refrigerate any unused portion.

Bleu Cheese Dressing

¾	Cup sour cream		⅓	Tsp. garlic powder
½	Tsp. dry mustard		1	Tsp. Worcestershire sauce
½	Tsp. black pepper		1 ⅓	Cups mayonnaise
½	Tsp. salt – scant		4	Oz. crumbled bleu cheese

In an electric mixing bowl, combine first 6 ingredients and blend at low speed. Add mayonnaise and continue to blend at low speed then increase speed to medium and blend an additional 2 minutes. Slowly add bleu cheese. Continue to blend if you wish or if you prefer a chunky dressing, fold in the bleu cheese. Refrigerate for 24 hours before serving. Refrigerate any unused portion.

Ginger Dressing

3	(½") Cubes ginger root – peeled & chopped		¼	Cup vinegar
			1	Onion – large & sliced
½	Cup soy sauce		2	Tsp. MSG

Place peeled and chopped ginger, soy sauce, vinegar, onion and MSG in blender. Blend at high speed two minutes or until ginger and onion are minced. Chill and serve with seafood. Refrigerate any unused dressing.

When you start having lunch
and actually eating,
it's already over
~Erica Jong

Braised Cabbage

* * * * *

*Ooops, be careful, this is my favorite and I love to entertain
using petite portions of several vegetables paired on the dinner plate
with the main event. You never want to be too full for dessert –
or too stuffed for later.*

¼ C	Peanut oil
1	Red onion – medium, sliced
1 C	Brown sugar – dark
2	Granny smith apples – sliced
½ C	Red wine vinegar
4 Lb.'s	Red cabbage – cut julienne
2 C	Red wine
2 C	Orange juice
1	Cinnamon stick
2 Tsp.	Ground ginger
	Salt & pepper – to taste

Heat a heavy oven proof skillet over medium high temperature. Add peanut oil and heat until temperature is ready to sauté the red onion until translucent. Reduce the heat and sprinkle in the brown sugar and cook for a few minutes until onions begin to caramelize. Add the sliced apples and deglaze the pan with the red wine vinegar. Bring to a boil. Stir in the red wine, orange juice, cinnamon stick, ginger, and salt & pepper. Simmer for 5 minutes. Add cabbage and continue to cook for about 10 minutes.

Cover cabbage with foil and place in 350 oven for about 45 minutes. Adjust the seasonings if necessary. Remove cinnamon stick before serving.

Note: If you do not have an oven proof skillet, you may prepare the first portion of the recipe in your regular skillet and then pour cabbage into a casserole dish for baking.

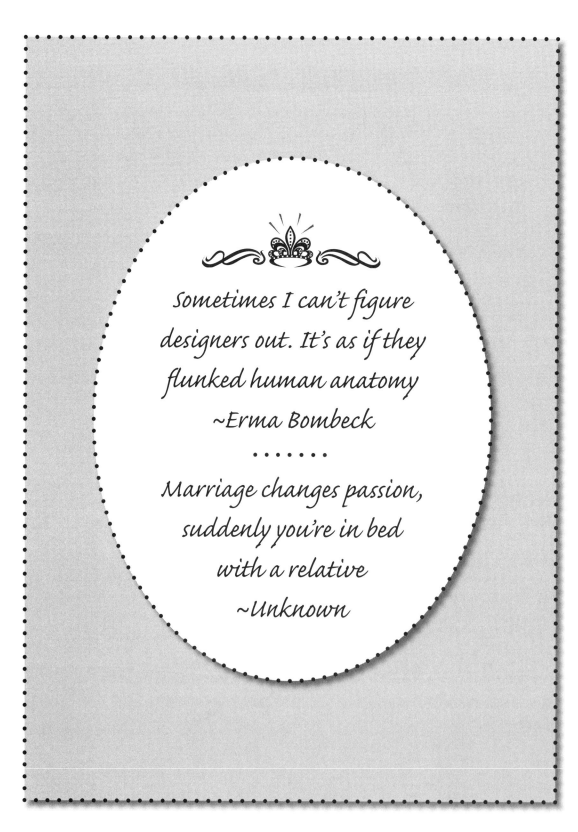

Sometimes I can't figure designers out. It's as if they flunked human anatomy

~Erma Bombeck

· · · · · · ·

Marriage changes passion, suddenly you're in bed with a relative

~Unknown

Twice Baked Sweet Potatoes

* * * * *

I made these for a funeral dinner – they were the talk of the event!

6	Lg. sweet potatoes or yams	½	Tsp. pepper
8	Oz. cream cheese – softened	½	Tsp. cinnamon
⅓	Cup brown sugar	⅓	Cup walnuts or pecans – chopped & sautéed in butter
2	Tbs. margarine		
1	Tbs. vanilla	½	Tsp. orange peel – grated
¾	Tsp. salt		

Bake potatoes at 375 for 45-60 minutes or until firm but tender. Remove from oven and cut off the top portion. Scoop out the potato leaving a ½ inch wall of potato to hold the mashed potatoes. Combine the scooped out sweet potatoes with cream cheese, margarine, brown sugar, vanilla, salt, pepper, orange peel, and cinnamon in a medium mixing bowl.

Stuff the potato shells and top with sautéed buttered nuts. You may also decorate with cinnamon stemmed cherries.

Scalloped Spinach

* * * * *

Fix this for the man "You" adore waking up next to in the morning.

1	10 Oz. frozen chopped spinach	½	Cup cheddar cheese
2	Tbs. onion – finely chopped	½	Cup buttered soft bread crumbs
2	Eggs – beaten	¼	Tsp. each salt & pepper
½	Cup milk		

Cook spinach according to package directions and drain completely. Add onion, eggs, milk and cheese. Add salt and pepper to taste. Place in buttered casserole dish and top with buttered soft bread crumbs. Bake in a preheated 350 oven for 20 minutes.

Don't settle for being a free
finishing school for men
~Suzanne Wolstenholme

. . . .

Sometimes love doesn't come
to us. We have to go out hunting.
It's like pigs looking for truffles.
It's called dating
~Patty LaPone

English Walnut Broccoli

* * * * *

This down home goodness will make His mama sit up,
take notice, and know you're a force to be reckoned with.

2-3	10 Oz. frozen broccoli – chopped	4	Tbs. flour
½	Cup butter	2	Cups milk
½	Tbs. powdered chicken stock base	8	Oz. herbed stuffing mix
		⅔	Cup walnuts – coarsley broken

Cook broccoli in salted water until tender. Drain and place in 9x12 baking dish. Melt butter, blend in flour and chicken stock. Gradually add milk stirring constantly until thick and smooth. Pour over broccoli. Heat ⅔ C water and 6Tbs. Butter. Remove stuffing mix from package and place in a medium bowl. Pour the water/butter mixture over and toss until coated. Add nuts and place on top of broccoli. Bake at 350 for 30 minutes.

Cranberry Wild Rice

* * * * *

There are many ways to bring your Uncle to the table
and this is one of my favorites.

1	Cup onion – chopped	2	6 Oz. pkg. Uncle Ben's long grain & wild rice
2	Tbs. butter		
1	Can whole cranberry sauce	1 ½	Cups celery – finely chopped

Cook onion and celery in butter till tender. Add enough water to cranberry sauce to make 4 ¼ cups. Add cranberry sauce to contents of rice and seasoning packet in skillet. Bring to boil, cover tightly and cook over low heat until liquid is absorbed.

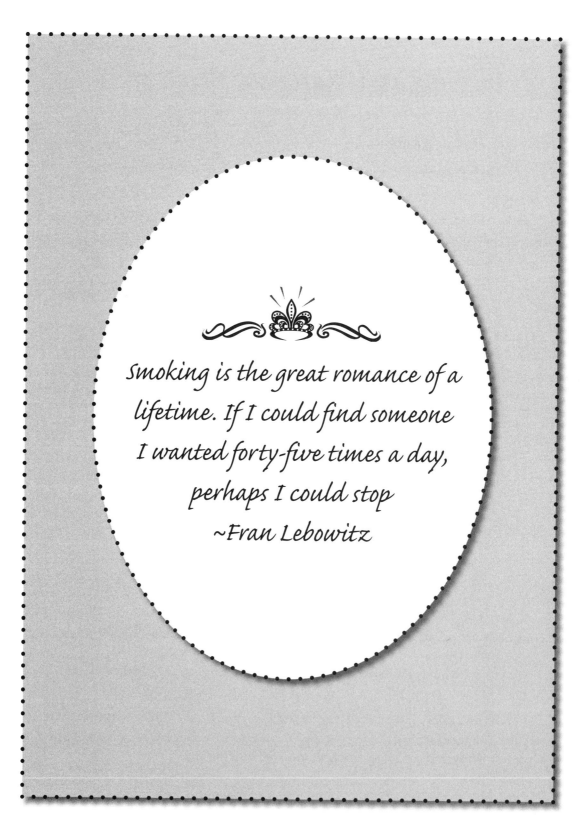

Smoking is the great romance of a lifetime. If I could find someone I wanted forty-five times a day, perhaps I could stop

~Fran Lebowitz

Turban Squash
* * * * *

If he asks you to go home for Thanksgiving to meet the family, don't take this!!!! They'll be jealous. Make this after you've hooked him.

1	3 lb. Turban squash	¼	Cup onion – chopped
1	Lb. sage flavored pork sausage	1	Egg – slightly beaten
1	Cup celery – chopped	½	Cup sour cream
½	Cup mushrooms – fresh & sliced	¼	Cup Parmesan cheese – grated
		¼	Tsp. salt

Cut slice from stem end of squash so it will stand upright. Cut out the turban end and scoop out seeds. Lightly salt inside and place squash scooped end down in shallow baking pan. Bake in 375 oven for 1 hour or until tender. Remove from oven and cool.

In skillet brown sausage, celery, mushrooms and onion until tender and lightly browned. Drain well. Add egg, sour cream, cheese and salt. Stir into sausage mixture. Turn squash scooped end up; fill with sausage mixture and bake at 350 for 20 to 25 minutes.

Connoisseur Casserole
* * * * *

Breaking all the diet rules won't hurt – just add a little elastic to your waist band dear!

1	12 Oz. Shoepeg corn – drained	1	10 ¾ Oz. cream of celery soup
1	16 Oz. French cut green beans– drained	½	Tsp. salt
½	Cup celery – chopped	½	Tsp. pepper
½	Cup onion – chopped		
1	2 Oz. pimientos – chopped		**Topping:**
½	Cup sour cream	1	Cup Ritz crackers – crushed
½	Cup sharp cheddar cheese – grated	¼	Cup butter – melted
		½	Cup slivered almonds

Combine all vegetables, sour cream, cheese, soup, salt and pepper in mixing bowl. Place in a greased 9x13 baking dish. In a smaller mixing bowl combine the topping. Sprinkle the topping over the vegetables and bake in a 350 oven for 45 minutes.

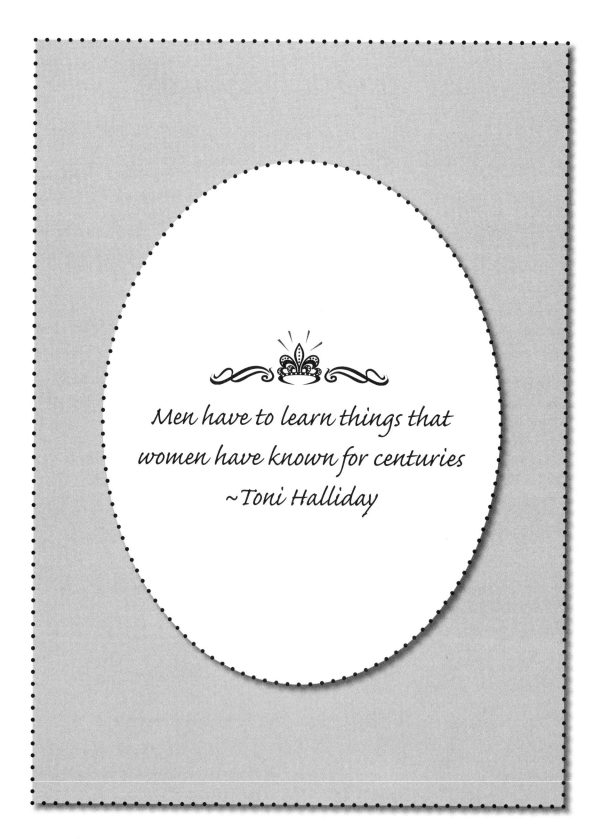

Men have to learn things that women have known for centuries

~Toni Halliday

Famous Baked Potatoes

* * * * *

Make these for that new man in your life. The mood you'll create will make him forget he ever had a mama, much less one that makes his favorite dinner.

8	Baking potatoes – scrubbed
3 Tbs.	Butter
4 C	Mushrooms – sliced
1 Tbs.	Chicken bouillon powder
¼ Tsp.	Garlic powder
¼ C	White Burgundy wine
1 ½ C	Swiss cheese – grated
1 ½ C	Ham – chopped
1 ¼ C	Sour cream
¼ C	Milk
	Salt & freshly ground pepper – to taste
¼ C	Butter – melted

Preheat oven to 400. Wrap potatoes in foil and bake until soft, about 1 hour. Let stand until cool enough to handle. Reduce oven temperature to 350.

Melt 3 Tbs. butter in a heavy skillet over medium heat. Add mushrooms and cook, stirring frequently, for 5 minutes. Stir in bouillon and garlic powder. Blend in wine and cook 1 minute longer.

Unwrap potatoes and discard foil. Slice off tops and set aside. Spoon cooked potato into large bowl and set skins aside. Add sautéed mushrooms, cheese, ham, sour cream and milk and blend well. Season with salt and pepper. Fill potato skins with mixture. Replace tops. Bake 15 minutes. Brush tops with melted butter and serve.

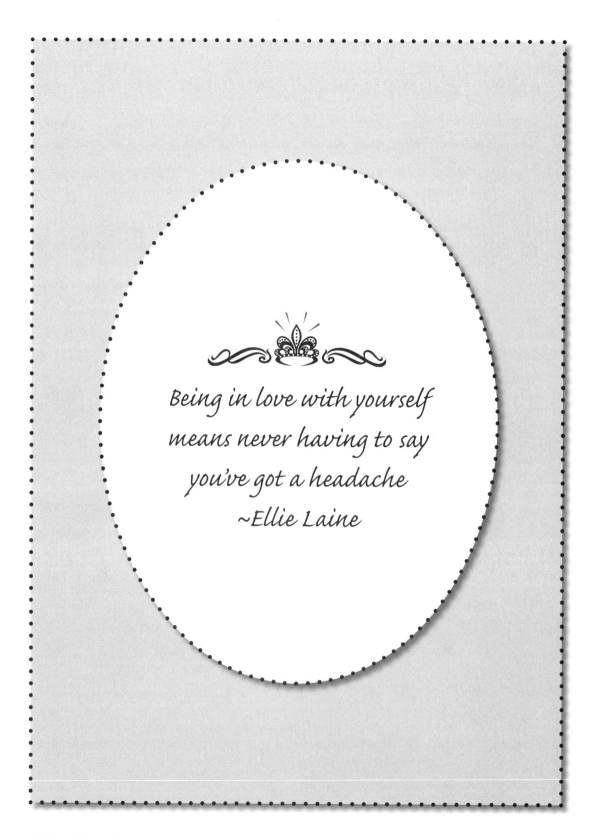

*Being in love with yourself
means never having to say
you've got a headache*
~Ellie Laine

Broccoli Creole

* * * * *

This is a show stopper (yes, more than the new teddy you're wearing)
on any dinner table. The color contrast is spectacular and
the taste truly pleases the palette.

2 Bunches	Fresh broccoli
4 Tbs.	Butter
½ C	Onion
1 C	Celery
2	Garlic cloves – chopped
1 C	Green pepper
2 C	Cherry tomatoes – halved
1 Tsp.	Salt
¼ Tsp.	Pepper
½ C	White wine
2 Tsp.	Cornstarch

Melt butter in 10 inch skillet. Add onion, celery, and garlic. Sauté until translucent. Season with salt and pepper. Add green pepper and tomatoes and continue to cook while keeping the green pepper and tomatoes intact and somewhat firm. The green pepper needs to be tender crisp. Add white wine and cook until the alcohol has evaporated. Add cornstarch if necessary.

Wash and trim broccoli. Place in 9x11 baking dish with stems pointing to center so that the green tops are on the outside of the casserole dish. Add 2 Tbs. water and cover with plastic wrap. Microwave until broccoli is tender crisp. About 10 minutes. Do not over cook or broccoli turns gray-green. When tender crisp, add Creole mixture down center. May be made ahead and reheated in 300 oven for 15 minutes.

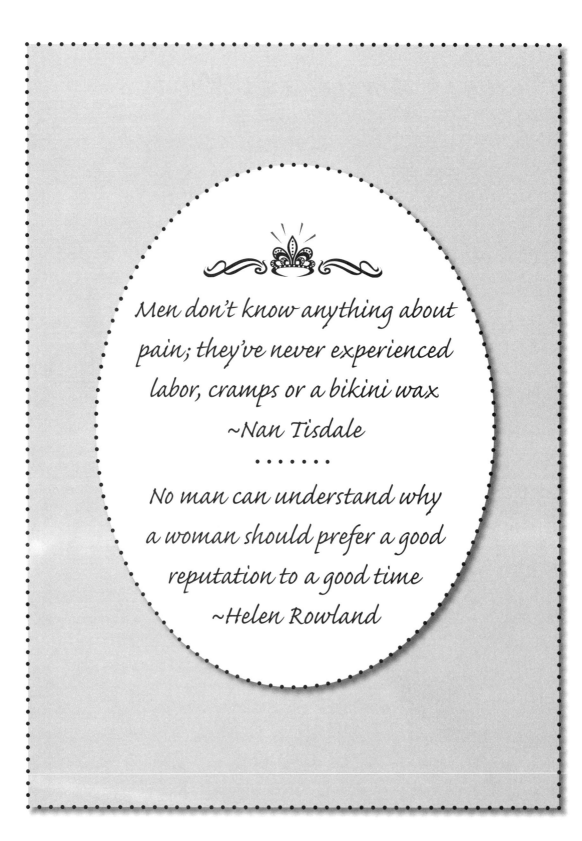

Men don't know anything about pain; they've never experienced labor, cramps or a bikini wax
~Nan Tisdale

. . . .

No man can understand why a woman should prefer a good reputation to a good time
~Helen Rowland

Roasted Red Potatoes

* * * * *

*These, along with a brisket, just scream for a
Sunday afternoon delight.*

Quarter enough small new potatoes to cover 9x12 baking dish. Dot with 1 stick butter, coarse salt, and fresh pepper. Bake in 400 oven tossing every 15-20 minutes so that potatoes are coated with butter and browning. The last 20 minutes of cooking add ¾ cup Worcestershire sauce and cover the potatoes. Continue to cook until sauce becomes a glaze over the potatoes. Total cooking will be approximately 1 hour.

Sweet Yellow Corn Pudding

* * * * *

Southern sweet and delicious – just enjoy the moment!

2 Cans	Whole kernel corn – drained
1 -14 ¾ Oz.	Creamed corn
10 Tbs.	Butter
¼ C	Sugar
5	Eggs – extra large & beaten
1 C	Flour
2 Tsp.	Baking powder
	Salt & Pepper – to taste
1 C	Sharp cheddar cheese – grated

In a large bowl combine both corns, butter, sugar, eggs, flour and baking powder. Season with salt and pepper and mix well. Pour into a buttered au gratin dish or 9x13 baking dish and bake 35-45 minutes at 350. Remove from oven and sprinkle cheese on top. Return to oven and bake for several more minutes until cheese is melted.

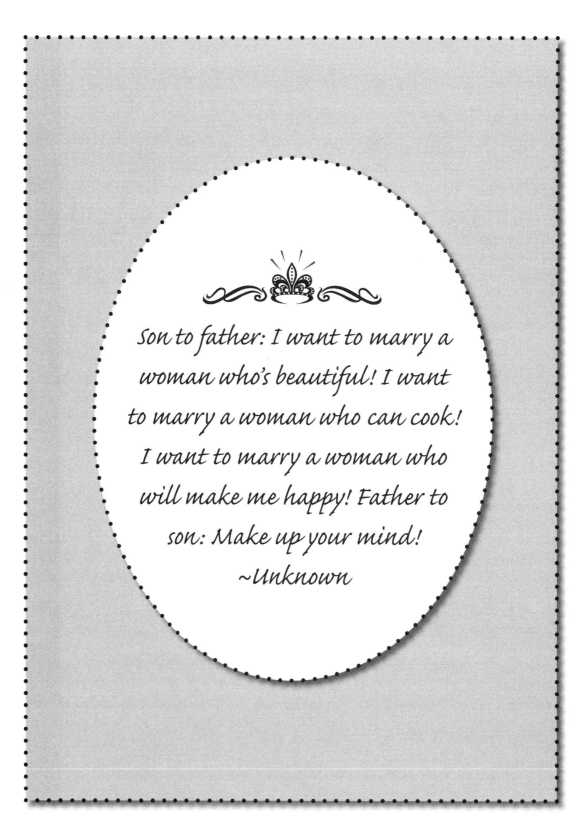

Son to father: I want to marry a woman who's beautiful! I want to marry a woman who can cook! I want to marry a woman who will make me happy! Father to son: Make up your mind!
~Unknown

Marinated Tomatoes

* * * * *

Exquisitely round and plumped to perfection, mixed with all the joys of every tomorrow (add Vidalia onions and cucumbers if you wish) then splashed with just the right amount of tartness for a suddenly summer sensation.

8	Tomatoes – large, firm, and peeled	½	Tsp. black pepper
½	Cup parsley – chopped	½	Cup olive oil
2	Garlic cloves – crushed	2	Tbs. red wine vinegar
2	Tsp. salt	2	Tbs. tarragon wine vinegar
2	Tsp. sugar	4	Tsp. prepared mustard

Cut peeled tomatoes into ½ inch slices and place in shallow serving dish. Combine parsley, garlic, salt, sugar, pepper, oil, red wine vinegar, tarragon wine vinegar and mustard in jar. Cover and shake well. Pour over tomatoes. Cover and chill. Let stand at room temperature at least 20 minutes before serving.

Baked Yams with Apples & Cranberries

* * * * *

There is an old saying, "if you eat a yam a day you won't get ill." Silly girl, you know our cure for all ills is a daily dose of peanut M&Ms.

1	Lg. apple – peeled, cored & diced	¼	Cup Orange liqueur (Triple Sec)
1	Bag cranberries – fresh	¾	Tsp. cinnamon
¾	Cup brown sugar	¼	Tsp. nutmeg
¾	Cup pecans – coarsely chopped	3	Medium-sized yams – peeled & sliced
½	Cup orange juice		

In a large bowl, combine apple, cranberries, sugar, pecans, orange juice, liqueur, cinnamon and nutmeg. Spread yams in a buttered 9x13 baking dish. Spoon apple mixture over. Cover with foil and bake at 400 for 45 minutes. Remove cover and bake 15 minutes more.

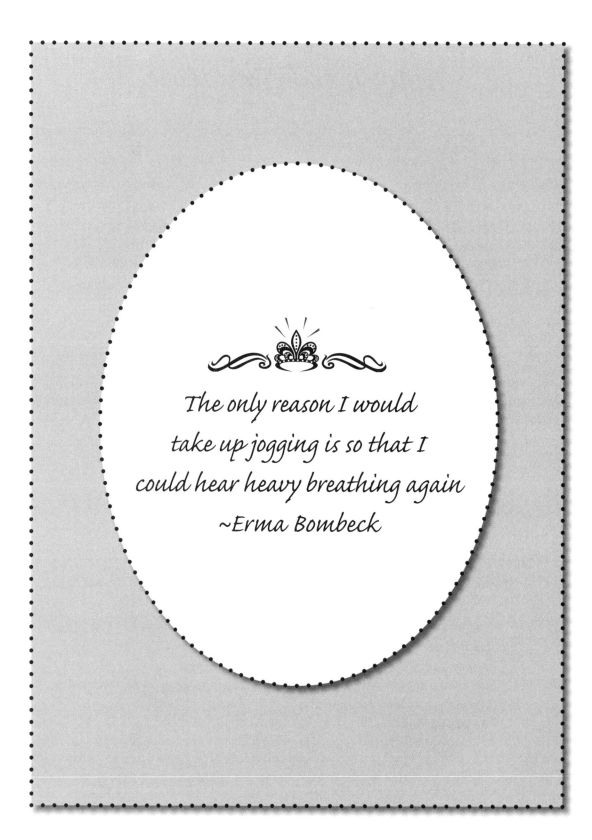

The only reason I would
take up jogging is so that I
could hear heavy breathing again
~Erma Bombeck

Coq-Au-Vin

* * * * *

We went to the boss's house for dinner and this was the main event.
His wife was a lovely lady willing to share with me. The recipe, my dear!

6	Chicken breasts (skinned & boned)	½	Tsp. thyme
3	Bacon slices – chopped fine & fried crisp.	1	Bay Leaf
1	Can silver skin onions – drained	1	Tsp. salt
			Grind of pepper
1	Garlic clove	3	Tbs. flour
6	Mushrooms – sliced	½	Cup red wine
¼	Cup cognac	1	Can beef consommé
		1	4 Oz. tomato sauce
		4	Tbs. whipping cream

Fry bacon in a large skillet. Remove bacon and all but 2 Tbs. of grease from pan, add a couple of tablespoons of oil. Fry chicken in remaining bacon grease and oil. Add onions, crushed garlic and sliced mushrooms. Sauté until soft. Heat cognac and pour over meat and flame. When flame burns out, add thyme, bay leaf, salt, pepper and flour. Mix well. Add red wine, consommé and the tomato sauce. Return bacon bits to pan. When ready to serve add whipping cream.

I have little feet because

nothing grows in the shade

~Dolly Parton

Bastille

* * * * *

*Go ahead, impress your girlfriends at a luncheon!
This one is sure to do it! It may take a little extra effort, but
it can be prepared weeks in advance, frozen, thawed and
reheated right before serving. Double the recipe and
use round disposable cake pans. It's a cinch!!*

1	1Lb. Phyllo Dough	½	Tsp. pepper
3½	Lb. chicken breast	12	Eggs – beaten
2	Cups water	1½	Cups butter – melted
2	Lemons – juiced	1	Cup slivered almonds
2	Onions – sliced	2	Tbs. sugar
1	Tsp. ginger		
1	Pinch saffron		**Topping:**
1	Cinnamon stick		Mix cinnamon & powdered sugar
1	Tsp. salt		

Defrost Phyllo dough. In a pot, simmer chicken in water with, lemon, onion, ginger, saffron, and cinnamon stick for 45 minutes or until tender. De-bone chicken and cut into bite sized pieces. Reduce liquid to 1 ½ C; discard cinnamon stick. Mix beaten eggs gradually into liquid until scrambled. Let cool. Brush 9" round cake pan with butter. Line pan with two layers of dough (buttering each layer). Put chicken in 1" layer and sprinkle with 2 Tsp. melted butter. Place two additional sheets of dough on top of chicken and brush with melted butter. Add egg mixture, then 2 more sheets of dough. Sprinkle almonds with 2 Tbs. sugar, 2 Tbs. melted butter. Fold over hanging sheets, then add two more sheets tucked in underneath. Brush top with butter. Bake for 30 minutes then turn over into baking sheet and continue baking for 15-25 minutes more or until top is crispy brown. Top with powdered sugar and cinnamon. Cut into wedges and serve immediately.

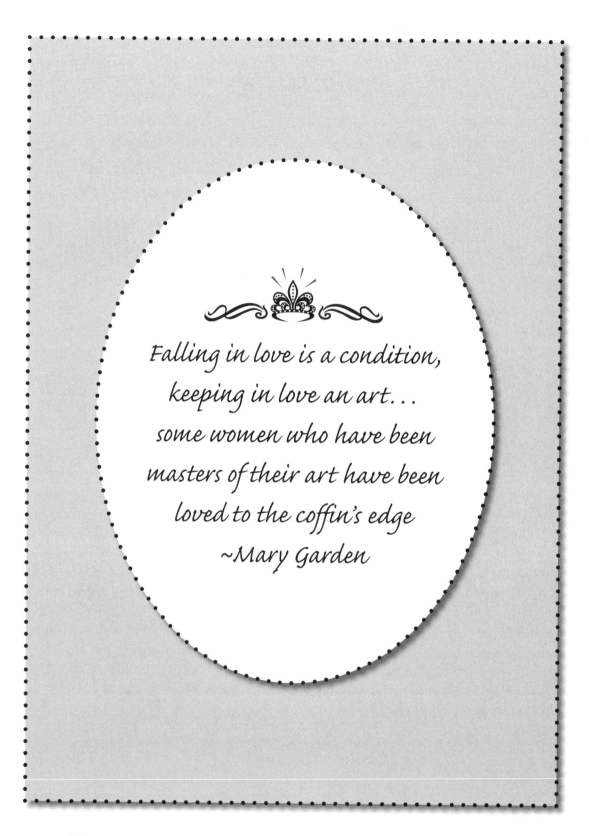

*Falling in love is a condition,
keeping in love an art…
some women who have been
masters of their art have been
loved to the coffin's edge
~Mary Garden*

Sweet & Sour Short Ribs
*****
*Is there anything in this recipe you just wouldn't love
to have licked off the back of your hand?*

Brush 2-3 Lbs. of short ribs with soy sauce and roast in 350 oven for 1 ¼ to 1 ½ hours. While the ribs are roasting, prepare the sauce.

Sauce:

1	Cup sugar	1	Tbs. cornstarch
1	Cup vinegar	1	Tbs. sugared ginger
½	Cup sherry wine	½	Cup pineapple chunks
2	Tbs soy sauce	¼	Cup sweet pickles
1	Green pepper – sliced		

Bring first 5 ingredients to a boil in a medium sauce pan. Add the cornstarch that has been mixed with water and dissolved. Stir until clear and thick. Add finely cut ginger, pineapple chunks and sweet pickles. Spoon over ribs after draining off fat. Continue to bake for an additional 20 minutes.

Beef Bourguignon
*****
*Candlelight dinner for two – this could be the clincher
for the "Will You......" proposal*

1	Lb. beef sirloin (lean) – cubed	1	Tsp. thyme
4	Tbs. butter	½	Tsp. freshly ground pepper
2	Cloves garlic – minced	½	Cup butter
1	Lb. mushrooms – sliced	½	Cup flour
2	Bay leaves (crushed)	1	Can beef consommé
2	Tbs. parsley – chopped	1 ½	Cans Burgundy – use the consommé can
1	Tsp. salt		

Heat butter in a large heavy skillet. Brown meat on all sides. Add garlic and mushrooms and continue to sauté until mushrooms are cooked. Season with spices. Transfer meat to Dutch oven. Melt the ½ cup butter in a large skillet and add flour to make a roux. Add consommé and burgundy wine cooking until thick. Pour over meat, cover and simmer 1 ½ hours or till meat is tender.

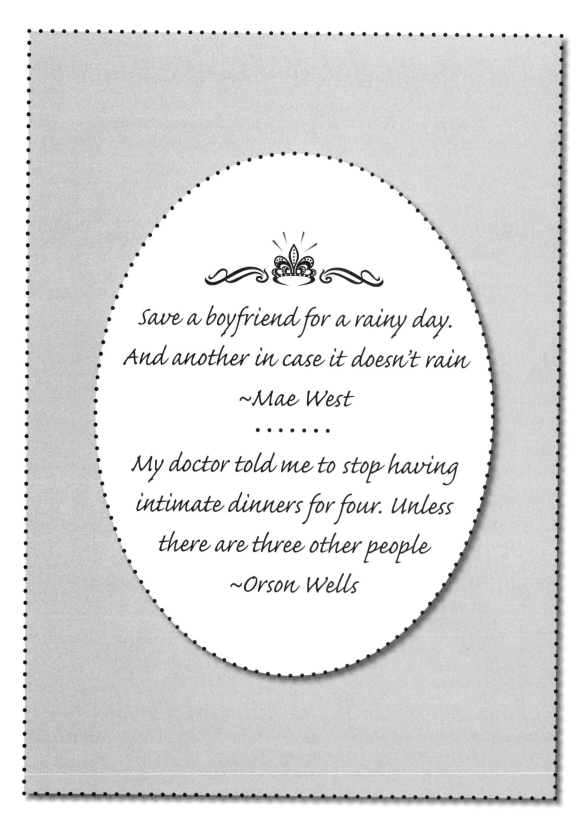

Save a boyfriend for a rainy day.
And another in case it doesn't rain

~Mae West

. . . .

My doctor told me to stop having
intimate dinners for four. Unless
there are three other people

~Orson Wells

Teriyaki Marinade

* * * * *

If boyfriend loves to grill, this recipe will bring the cows a calling,
the chickens roosting, and the pigs a flying home to
lay down on the "barbie."

⅔	Cup soy sauce	2	Tsp. ginger – fresh & grated
¼	Cup salad oil	2	Tsp. dry mustard
2	Tbs. molasses	6	Garlic cloves – minced

Combine all ingredients. This is enough for 2 Lb.'s of meat. Marinate overnight in the refrigerator or at room temperature for 3 hours. Ready for the grill.

Grilled Ham Marinade

* * * * *

There's not a butt, loin, or ham that won't love getting soaked
in this combination. Absolutely the best --- but remember,
use only Canada Dry. Don't be cheap! It won't be as tasty!
Take it from one who found out the hard way.

½	Cup ginger ale	½	Cup orange juice
¼	Cup brown sugar	1	Tbs. Canola oil
1 ½	Tsp. white wine vinegar	1	Tsp. dry mustard
¼	Tsp. ground ginger	⅛	Tsp. ground cloves

Combine all ingredients and add ham steak. Marinate overnight and grill till heated through. May also use as a pork chop marinade.

When we lose, I eat.
When we win, I eat. I also eat
when we're rained out
~Tommy Lasorda

Stuffed Rigatoni

* * * * *

Worth every minute of effort – that's all I can say.
Even your best friends' husband will be impressed!

¼ C	Olive oil
1 Lg.	Onion – chopped
2	Garlic cloves – minced
1 Lb.	Ground beef
¼ Lb.	Ground pork
2 Tbs.	Fresh parsley
¼ Tsp.	Italian seasonings
	Salt & pepper – to taste
2 Pkgs.	Spinach – chopped frozen
¾ C	Parmesan cheese – grated
1 C	Bread crumbs
2	Eggs

Heat oil in large skillet and add onion and garlic to sauté. Add ground beef and pork and continue to cook until meat looses its pink. Do not brown. Add the parsley, Italian seasonings, salt and pepper. Meanwhile, microwave the spinach to defrost. Drain and squeeze all liquid out of the spinach; then chop more. Add to the cooked meat mixture along with the cheese, bread crumbs and 2 eggs.

In large sauce pan cook rigatoni noodles in boiling water until barely limp. Drain and cover with cold water to avoid sticking. Stuff meat mixture into rigatoni and lay in rows in a flat 9x13 baking dish. Top with your favorite spaghetti sauce, parmesan cheese and mozzarella cheese. Bake covered 40 minutes in 325 oven.

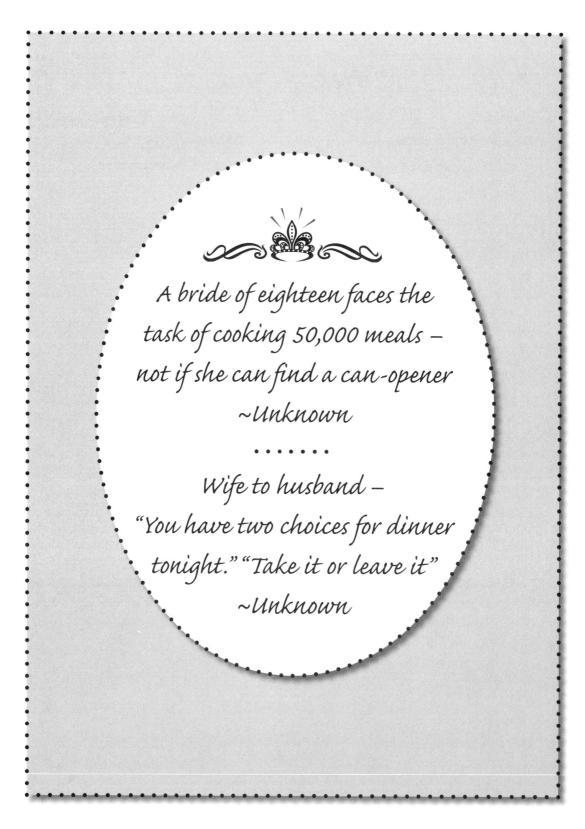

A bride of eighteen faces the task of cooking 50,000 meals – not if she can find a can-opener
~Unknown

. . . .

Wife to husband – "You have two choices for dinner tonight." "Take it or leave it"
~Unknown

Tenderloin Tips in Burgundy Wine

* * * * *

I love anything with red wine – a good excuse to open a bottle!

6	Tbs. butter	1 ¼	Cups brown beef gravy – commercial
1 ½	Lb. beef tenderloin – cut in thin stripes	1	Cup Burgundy wine
2	Med. onion – chopped	2	Tbs. cornstarch
2	Green pepper – chopped		

In a large heavy skillet sauté meat in 2 Tbs. butter. Add remaining butter and sauté vegetables until they are tender crisp and meat is cooked to medium. In a small bowl add gravy and wine into cornstarch stirring until dissolved. Add beef mixture and continue to cook, stirring constantly, until mixture bubbles, then cook 2 minutes longer. Serve over hot buttered egg noodles.

Turkey Tetrazzinni

* * * * *

If you want to please your son and see your daughter-in-law sparkle, ask her for her specialty recipe. This is my daughter-in-law's favorite and we always request it when we visit their home.

¼	Cup butter	3	Cups spaghetti – cooked
¼	Cup flour	2	Cups turkey – cut into bite sized pieces
1	Tsp. chicken bouillon	1	Can mushrooms – sliced
1	Tsp. salt	1	Tbs. parsley
¼	Tsp. pepper	2	Tbs. sherry
½	Cup water	2	Tbs. parmesan cheese
1 ½	Cups whipping cream	1	Cup cheddar cheese – shredded

Melt butter and add flour to make a roux. Sprinkle with bouillon, salt, pepper and hot water. Stir until thick and bubbly. Add cream, turkey, mushrooms, parsley, and sherry. Mix with spaghetti and turn into a 9x13 prepared baking dish. Sprinkle with cheeses and bake at 350 for 30-40 minutes until heated through and bubbly.

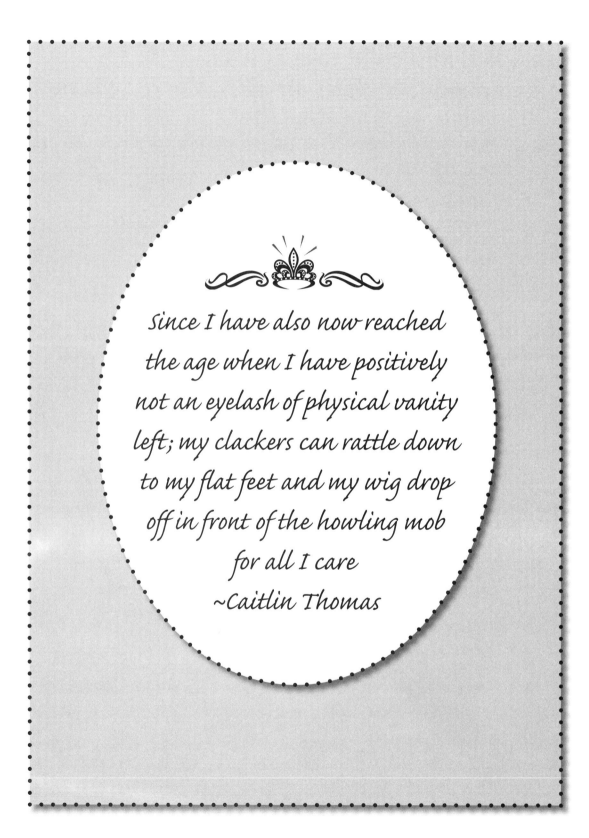

Since I have also now reached
the age when I have positively
not an eyelash of physical vanity
left; my clackers can rattle down
to my flat feet and my wig drop
off in front of the howling mob
for all I care
~Caitlin Thomas

Artichoke Chicken

* * * * *

Oh my, what chicken wouldn't just love to get drenched in all the goodness of these ingredients. I'd be tempted to jump in myself!

8	Chicken breasts – skinless & boneless	⅓	Cup flour
2	Tbs. butter	1 ½	Tsp. rosemary
2	6 Oz. jar marinated artichoke hearts – drained	1	Tsp. salt
		¼	Tsp. pepper
1	4 ½ Oz. jar whole mushrooms	1	Cup dry white wine
½	Cup onion – chopped	1	Cup chicken broth
			Fresh parsley

In a skillet, brown chicken in butter. Remove chicken to an ungreased 9x13 baking dish; do not drain pan juices. Cut the artichokes into quarters. Arrange artichokes and mushrooms on top of chicken; set aside. Sauté onion in pan juices; blend in flour, rosemary, salt and pepper. Add chicken broth; cook until thickened and bubbly. Remove from the heat and spoon over chicken. Cover and bake at 350 for 50-60 minutes or until chicken is tender. Place noodles on serving platter; top with chicken and sauce. Sprinkle with parsley.

Baked Chicken Salad

* * * * *

A wonderful Christmas luncheon favorite of the ladies with "0" calories. Courtesy of the great bearded wonder – Santa!!!!

3	Cups diced chicken	2	Tbs. onion – chopped
2	Cups celery – diced	½	Cup mayonnaise
½	Cup almonds – toasted	2	Tbs. lemon juice
½	Cup green pepper – diced	½	Cup cream of chicken soup
2	Tbs. pimentos	½	Cup sharp cheddar cheese – grated
½	Tsp. salt		

Combine all of the above ingredients in a 9x13 greased casserole. Sprinkle with crushed corn flakes that have been mixed with ¼ C melted butter. Bake at 350 for 30 minutes.

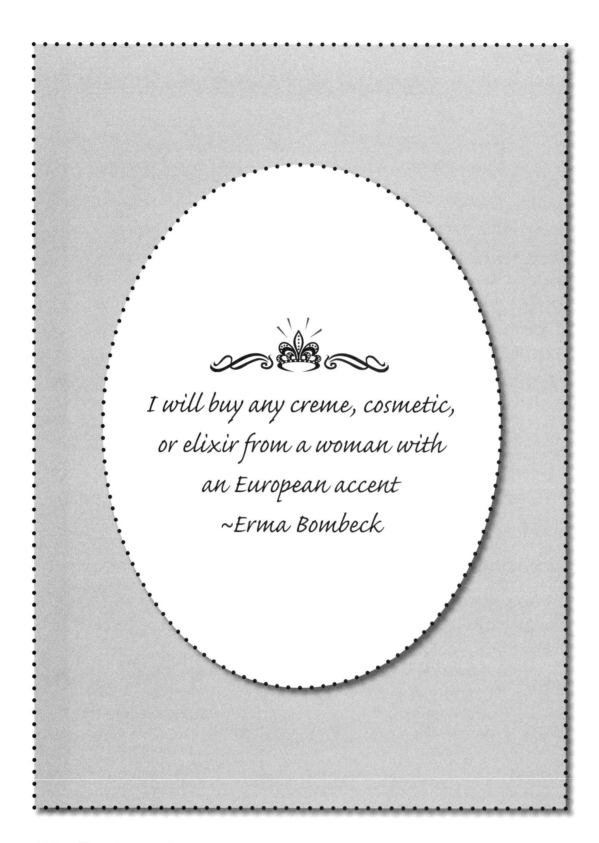

I will buy any creme, cosmetic,
or elixir from a woman with
an European accent
~Erma Bombeck

Double Good Manicotti

* * * * *

My son and his wife were the proud parents of a new baby girl.
This dish was their welcome home dinner. Simply sensational!!!

1	Lg. onion – chopped	1	Lb. ground beef
1	Garlic clove – minced	½	Cup walnuts – chopped
2	Tbs. butter	2	Eggs
1	Tbs. Italian seasonings	1	Pkg. spinach – frozen chopped – (thawed and drained)
2 ½	Tsp. salt	1 ½	Cups cream-style cottage cheese
1	Tsp. sugar	1	Pkg. cream cheese (3-4oz.)
4	8 Oz. tomato sauce	1	Pkg. mozzarella cheese – sliced (8oz.)
1	Can Italian tomatoes		
1	Pkg. Manicotti noodles		

Cook manicotti noodles, a few at a time, in a large amount of boiling salted water, following label directions; lift out carefully with a slotted spoon. Place in a pan of cold water until ready to fill.

Sauté onion and garlic in butter just until onion is soft in a medium-size saucepan; stir in Italian seasoning, 1 Tsp. of the salt, sugar, tomato sauce, and tomatoes. Simmer, stirring several times.

In a medium skillet, sauté ground beef until lightly browned. Add walnuts, 1 of the eggs and ½ of the spinach and 1 Tsp. of the salt. Blend cottage cheese with cream cheese, remaining ½ Tsp. salt, 1 egg, and spinach in a medium-size bowl. Remove noodles from water and drain well. Fill ½ of the noodles with the meat mixture and the other ½ with the cheese mixture, using a long-handled teaspoon.

Spoon 2 cups of the hot tomato sauce into a buttered baking pan; arrange filled noodles on top; spoon remaining sauce over; cover. Bake at 350 for 30 minutes uncovered. Arrange mozzarella slices overlapping on top. Bake an additional 10 minutes longer or until cheese melts.

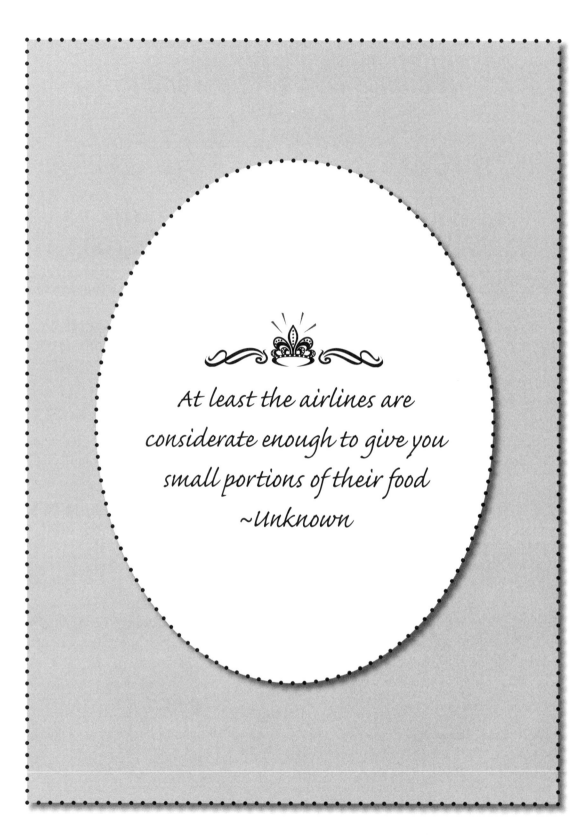

*At least the airlines are
considerate enough to give you
small portions of their food
~Unknown*

Ham-Stuffed Manicotti

* * * * *

Every sensation will be aroused when his lips savor the first bite.
He will only have eyes for you.

8	Manicotti shells
½ C	Onion – chopped
1 Tbs.	Oil
3 C	Ham – fully cooked & ground
1 Can	Mushrooms – sliced (4 oz.)
1 C	Swiss cheese – shredded
3 Tbs.	Grated parmesan cheese
½ C	Green pepper – chopped
3 Tbs.	Butter
3 Tbs.	Flour
2 C	Milk
	Parsley – for color

Cook manicotti according to package directions; set aside. In a large skillet, sauté onion in oil until tender. Remove from the heat. Add ham, mushrooms, ½ of the Swiss cheese and Parmesan; set aside. In a saucepan, sauté green pepper in butter until tender. Stir in flour until thoroughly combined. Add milk; cook, stirring constantly, until thickened and bubbly. Mix ¼ of the sauce into ham mixture. Stuff shells with about ⅓ cup of filling each. Place in a greased 7x11 baking dish. Top with remaining sauce; sprinkle with paprika. Cover and bake at 350 for 30 minutes or until heated through. Sprinkle with parsley and remaining Swiss cheese before serving.

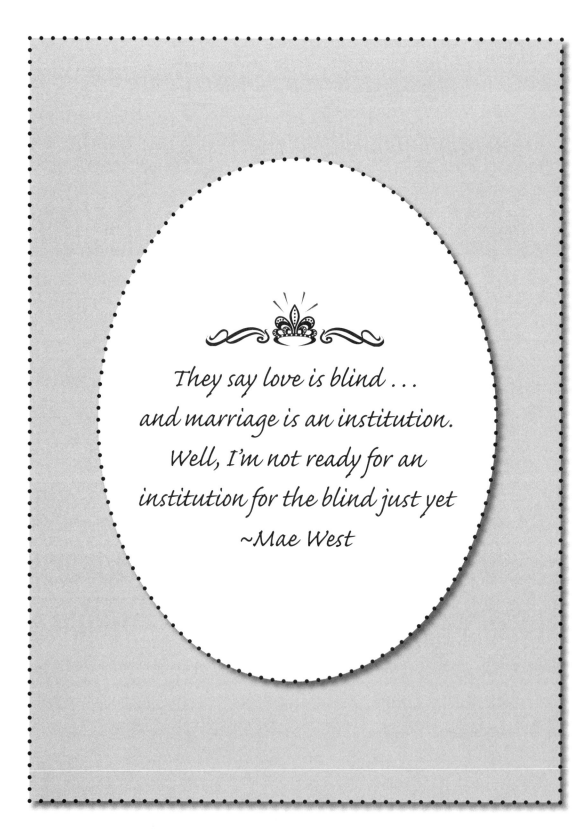

They say love is blind . . .
and marriage is an institution.
Well, I'm not ready for an
institution for the blind just yet
~Mae West

Pumpkin Stew

* * * * *

A grand presentation with an earthy flavor. This was a surprise delight at a family dinner. My grandchildren couldn't believe that you could actually eat right out of a pumpkin. A crowd pleaser during the season.

2 Lb.'s	Beef stew meat – cut into 1-inch cubes
3 Tbs.	Oil
1 C	Water
3	Potatoes – peeled & cut into 1-inch cubes
4	Carrots – sliced
1	Green pepper – cut into ½ inch pieces
4	Garlic cloves – minced
1	Onion – chopped
2 Tsp.	Salt
½ Tsp.	Pepper
2 Tbs.	Beef bouillon – instant granules
1-14 ½ Oz.	Tomatoes – diced
1	Pumpkin – 10-12 lb. size

In a Dutch oven, brown meat in 2 Tbs. oil. Add water, potatoes, carrots, green pepper, garlic, onion, salt and pepper. Cover and simmer for 2 hours. Stir in bouillon and tomatoes. Wash pumpkin; cut a 6- to 8-inch circle around top stem. Remove top and set aside; discard seeds and loose fibers from inside. Place pumpkin in a shallow sturdy baking pan. Spoon stew into pumpkin and replace the top. Brush outside of pumpkin with remaining oil. Bake at 325 for 2 hours or just until the pumpkin is tender (do not over bake). Serve stew from pumpkin, scooping out a little pumpkin with each serving.

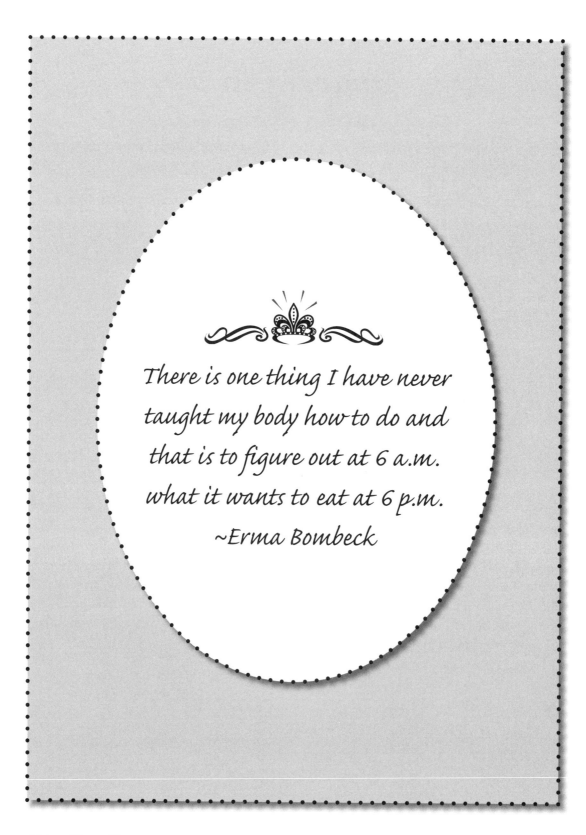

There is one thing I have never taught my body how to do and that is to figure out at 6 a.m. what it wants to eat at 6 p.m.

~Erma Bombeck

Pecan Crusted Filet Mignon

* * * * *

There should always be one truly special dish for entertaining in your treasure chest of recipes. Elegant and simple preparations with make-ahead ease can give you the freedom to enjoy all of life's other pleasures.

½ C	Pecans – toasted
½ C	Flour
1	Whole filet mignon – trimmed
	Vegetable oil
½ C	Dijon mustard
	Salt & pepper – to taste

Preheat oven to 375. Puree pecans in food processor until mealy in texture. Add the flour and pulse until incorporated with the pecans. Season the filet mignon with the salt and pepper. Sear the filet in hot vegetable oil until it has a rich brown color, turning to brown all sides. Remove from the pan and let it cool for a few minutes. Brush the filet with light coat of Dijon mustard, using a pastry brush. Pack the pecan and flour mixture on the filet and sauté in fresh oil until golden brown on all sides. Place the filet on a rack and finish roasting for approximately 10 minutes. Serve with the Port Wine Sauce.

Port Wine Sauce:

½ C	Shallots – chopped
3 Tbs.	Butter
1 Tbs.	Peppercorns
6 Oz.	Port wine
⅛ C	Balsamic vinegar
¼ Bunch	Fresh thyme leaves
1 ½ Qt.	Demi-glaze'

Sweat shallots in 2 ounces of butter. Add the peppercorns, wine and vinegar. Reduce the wine slightly. Add the demi-glaze' and simmer until it reduces and becomes thick. Serve over filet.

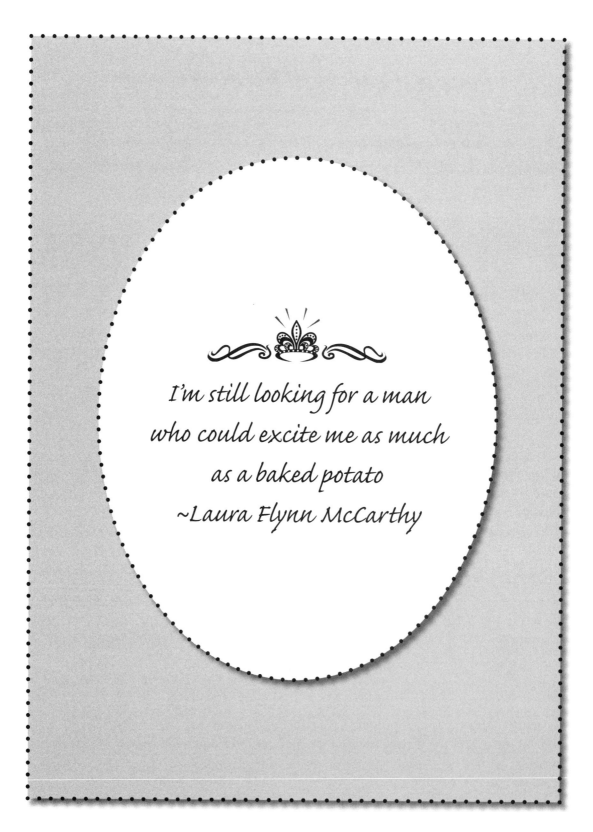

*I'm still looking for a man
who could excite me as much
as a baked potato
~Laura Flynn McCarthy*

Penne with Sausage, Peas & Mascarpone

* * * * *

Crusty bread, a bottle of wine and thou – makes me quiver.

¾ Lb.	Hot Italian sausages – casings removed
¾ Lb.	Sweet Italian sausages – casings removed
1 C	Onion – chopped
1 ¼ C	Whipping cream
¾ C	Chicken broth
1 Lb.	Penne pasta
2 C	Frozen peas
⅔ C	Mascarpone cheese
¾ C	Freshly grated Parmesan cheese

Sauté sausages in Dutch oven over high heat until brown, breaking into small pieces with back of spoon. Transfer to bowl. Pour off all but 1 Tbs. sausage drippings. Add onion and sauté until light brown. Add cream; boil 5 minutes. Add broth; boil until reduced to sauce consistency, stirring occasionally, about 8 minutes. Return sausage to pot.

Cook penne in large pot of boiling salted water until pasta is just tender. Meanwhile, bring sauce to simmer over medium heat. Add peas and mascarpone; simmer until peas are tender, about 6 minutes.

Drain pasta. Add to sauce; toss to coat. Mix in Parmesan. Season with salt and pepper. Transfer to large bowl and serve.

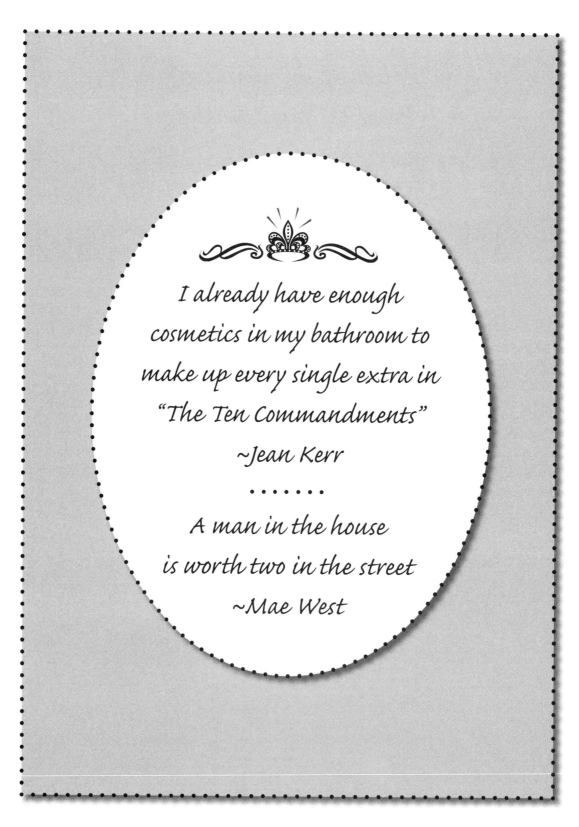

*I already have enough
cosmetics in my bathroom to
make up every single extra in
"The Ten Commandments"
~Jean Kerr*

. . . .

*A man in the house
is worth two in the street
~Mae West*

Coca-Cola Brisket

* * * * *

You clamor for anything slow and easy during a snowy winter weekend. A heavenly comfort food.

1	4 Lb. beef brisket	2	Garlic cloves – crushed
2	Tbs. oil	½	Cup ketchup
1	Cup onion – chopped	¼	Cup hot water
1	Cup celery – chopped	1	Tbs. onion soup powder
	Salt & pepper	1	Pkg. spaghetti sauce mix – dry
2	Tsp. paprika	1	Cup Coca-Cola

Place meat in large roasting pan and coat with oil on all sides. Sprinkle with onions and celery. Season with salt and pepper to taste and paprika. Place crushed garlic on top.

Mix ketchup with hot water; onion soup powder and dry spaghetti sauce mix to dissolve dry ingredients. Add cola and pour mixture over meat.

Cover with foil and roast at 350 degrees until very tender, 2 ½ to 3 hours, opening to baste with pan juices every 20 to 30 minutes. Slice and serve immediately, or slice, refrigerate and reheat in gravy next day. (30 minutes in a 350 degree oven for extra tender slices.)

Bavarian Pot Roast

* * * * *

There is only one thing better than eating this and that is being there.

1	3 Lb. pot roast – boneless	2	Tbs. sugar
2	Tbs. oil	1	Tbs. vinegar
1 ¼	Cup water	2	Tsp. salt
¾	Cup beer	1	Tsp. cinnamon
1	8 Oz. tomato sauce	½	Tsp. pepper
½	Cup onion – chopped	½	Tsp. ground ginger

In Dutch oven on top of stove, heat oil and place roast in pan and brown on both sides. Combine water, beer, tomato sauce, onion, sugar, vinegar and remaining spices in medium mixing bowl until thoroughly mixed. Pour over meat. Place Dutch oven in a 350 oven and bake until fork tender. Approximately 1 ½ to 2 hours.

Pan juices may be strained and mixed with 1 to 2 Tbs. of cornstarch. Heat on top of stove to a boil and gravy is thickened. Pour over sliced meat.

When I found out we are
what we eat, I stopped eatin'
pig cracklins and sow belly
~Judy Canova

Smothered Pork Chops with Blue Cheese-Applejack Gravy

* * * * *

We love it when Miss Piggy makes her grand entrance
at our dinner table. A succulent extraordinary sauce
completes this masterpiece.

8	Bacon slices – chopped
2	Onions – thinly sliced
2	Granny Smith apples – peeled, cored & each cut into 8 wedges
1 Tbs.	Sugar
2 Tbs.	Flour
1 C	Apple juice
1 C	Chicken broth
½ C	Applejack or other apple brandy
1 C	Crumbled Maytag bleu cheese
4 -6 Oz.	Pork loin chops

Cook bacon in heavy large skillet over medium heat until crisp. Transfer to paper towels. Spoon off 1 Tbs. drippings from skillet and reserve; discard all but 2 Tbs. remaining drippings in skillet. Add onions to skillet and sauté until golden, about 15 minutes. Push onions to side of skillet; add apples and sugar to skillet. Sauté until apples are golden, about 20 minutes. Transfer mixture to bowl.

Heat 1 Tbs. reserved bacon drippings in same skillet. Add flour and stir 1 minute. Gradually whisk in juice, broth and applejack. Boil until gravy thickens, whisking frequently, about 4 minutes. Add cheese and whisk until melted. Season with salt and pepper. Add onion mixture to gravy and stir until heated through. Remove from heat. Cover and keep warm.

Season pork with salt and pepper. Heat large nonstick skillet over medium heat. Add pork and sauté until cooked through, about 6 minutes per side. Transfer to bowl. Pour gravy over. Top with bacon and serve.

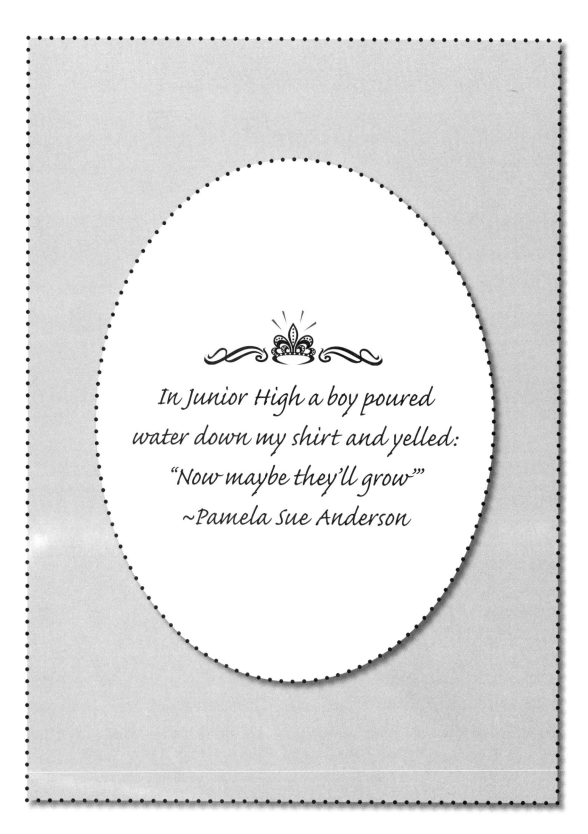

In Junior High a boy poured
water down my shirt and yelled:
"Now maybe they'll grow'"
~Pamela Sue Anderson

Chicken with Couscous
& Sage Cream Sauce
* * * * *

There are foods that you can just rub on your thighs. But remember, if you eat standing up, the calories all go to your feet and you can walk them off.

6	Boneless skinless chicken breast halves	¼	Cup lemon juice
	Salt & pepper – to taste		Couscous
2	Garlic cloves – crushed	6	Sprigs sage
			Sage Cream Sauce

Place chicken breasts in shallow pan. Season to taste with salt and pepper on both sides. Rub with garlic and brush with lemon juice. Cover and marinate several hours or overnight in refrigerator.

When ready to use, prepare Couscous and Sage Cream Sauce. Grill chicken breasts over medium coals or under broiler until done on both sides. For each serving, spoon some couscous onto plate and arrange 1 chicken breast over couscous. Pour ¼ C sage cream sauce over each serving of chicken. Garnish with 1 sprig of sage.

1	10 Oz. pkg. couscous	¼	Cup butter
	Water		Salt & pepper – to taste
1 ½	Cup chicken broth		

Place couscous in bowl with water to cover. Let soak 10 minutes. Drain excess water. Bring chicken broth and butter to boil in saucepan. Add couscous and season to taste with salt and pepper. Stir until broth is absorbed. Cover pan and remove from heat. Let stand 5 minutes. Fluff couscous lightly with fork.

Sage Cream Sauce:

1	Qt. whipping cream	2	Tbs. white wine
½	Tsp. chicken base granules or powder	1	Bunch sage – chopped
			Salt & pepper – to taste
1	Tsp. lemon juice		

Bring cream to boil and cook over medium-high heat until reduced by half. Add chicken base, lemon juice, wine and sage. Place mixture in blender container and blend until smooth. Season to taste with salt and pepper.

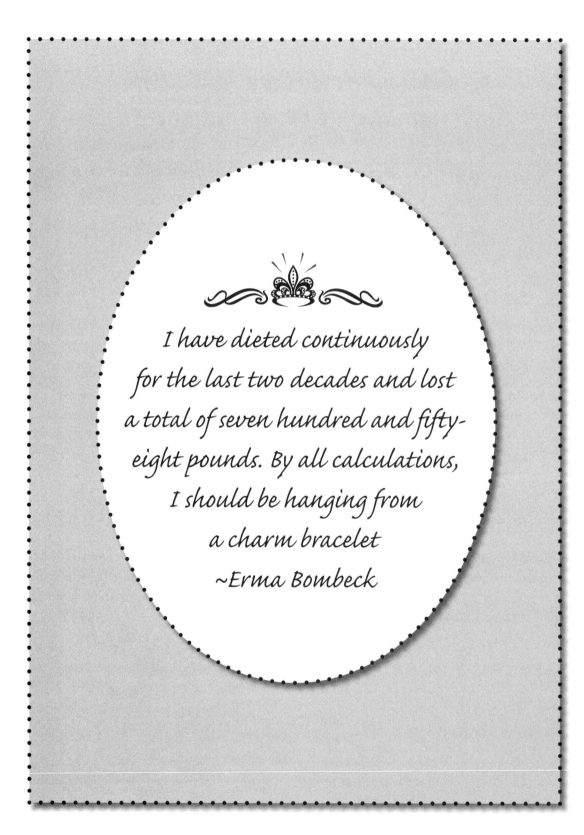

*I have dieted continuously
for the last two decades and lost
a total of seven hundred and fifty-
eight pounds. By all calculations,
I should be hanging from
a charm bracelet
~Erma Bombeck*

Cranberry Pork Roast

* * * * *

*Be an explorer of good food and let this be the
crowning glory on your holiday table.*

2 ½ -3	Lb. pork roast – boneless & frozen		1	Tsp. dry mustard
1	Can jellied whole cranberry sauce		¼	Tsp. ground cloves
			2	Tbs. cornstarch
½	Cup sugar		2	Tbs. cold water
½	Cup cranberry juice			Salt & pepper – to taste

Place frozen pork roast in your favorite roasting pan. In bowl, mash the cranberry sauce, sugar, juice, mustard and cloves. Pour over roast, cover and cook in 250 oven for 3-4 hours or until tender. Pour juice into saucepan and skim fat. Add enough water to make 2 cups. Combine cornstarch and 2 Tbs. cold water. Add slurry to saucepan. Cook stirring constantly until gravy thickens. Season with salt and pepper. Serve over sliced pork.

Pork Medallions with Green Peppercorn Sauce

* * * * *

When you want to go for the gold – you'll win a medal with this one!

1 ½	Lb. pork tenderloins		1	Tbs. peppercorns – drained
3	Tbs. butter		1 ½	Tsp. fresh thyme – minced
2	Shallots – minced		2	Tsp. Dijon mustard
½	Cup dry vermouth		⅓	Cup whipping cream
1 ½	Cups chicken stock			Fresh thyme leaves

Flatten pork slightly. Season with salt and pepper. Melt 2 Tbs. butter in large skillet at medium heat. Brown pork 3 minutes per side. Transfer to plate. Melt 1 Tbs. butter in same skillet. Add shallots and sauté 2 minutes. Add vermouth and boil until reduced to glaze. Add stock, peppercorns and thyme. Boil 10 minutes. Whisk in mustard, then cream. Add pork and simmer until done and sauce thickens slightly. Sprinkle with fresh thyme.

Feed me with your love –
your raisins and your apples
for I am utterly lovesick
~Song of Songs

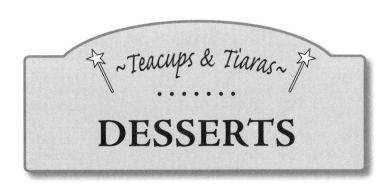

~Teacups & Tiaras~

DESSERTS

Dutch Apple Pie

* * * * *

This takes me down memory lane — the fragrance of going home.

8	Apples – sliced
1 ½ C	Sugar – 2 cups if apples are tart
3 Tbs.	Flour
1 Tsp.	Cinnamon
1 C	Whipping cream

Toss together the peeled, cored, and sliced apples, sugar, flour and cinnamon. Place in a single pie crust and rest on oven rack. Pour the whipping cream over apples and bake for one hour in a 400 oven. If necessary, the last 20 minutes, you may place foil around pie crust to cover and prevent over browning.

Note: You may use Granny Smith, Jonathan, or any other good baking apple.

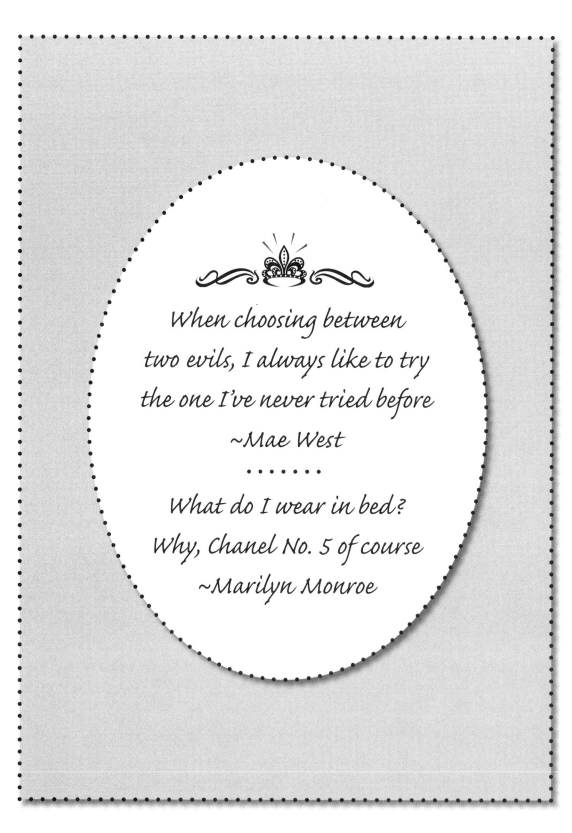

When choosing between
two evils, I always like to try
the one I've never tried before
~Mae West

. . . .

What do I wear in bed?
Why, Chanel No. 5 of course
~Marilyn Monroe

Rhubarb Torte

* * * * *

Pure pucker power and sinfully delicious as well.

1	Cup flour	¼	Tsp. salt
2	Tbs. sugar	½	Cup butter – melted

Blend above ingredients and pat into an 8 x 8 pan. Bake for 30 min. at 325.

1 ¼	Cups sugar	2	Tbs. flour
2 ¼	Cups rhubarb	½	Cup cream
3	Egg yolks		

Combine ingredients and place over baked crust. Return to oven and continue baking at 350 for 40 minutes. Whip the three egg whites with 3 Tbs. sugar until stiff. Cover baked torte and return to oven to brown for about 15 minutes at 350.

Sour Cream Raisin Pie

* * * * *

*Just like mother's milk – **real** sour whipping cream is the secret.*

1	Single crust baked pie shell	2	Egg yolks
1	Cup raisins	¾	Cup brown & white sugar – mixed
1	Cup hot boiling water – let raisins soak until plump	2	Tbs. flour – heaping
1	Cup sour cream	½	Tsp. Cinnamon

While raisins are plumping in boiling water, combine sour cream, egg yolks, sugars, flour and cinnamon and cook over medium heat until thick and flour is cooked. Drain raisins and add to pudding mixture. Cool and place in baked pie crust.

Beat two egg whites until stiff. Add two Tbs. of sugar and one Tsp. of cream of tarter. Arrange on top of cooled pie. Return to 350 oven and brown topping.

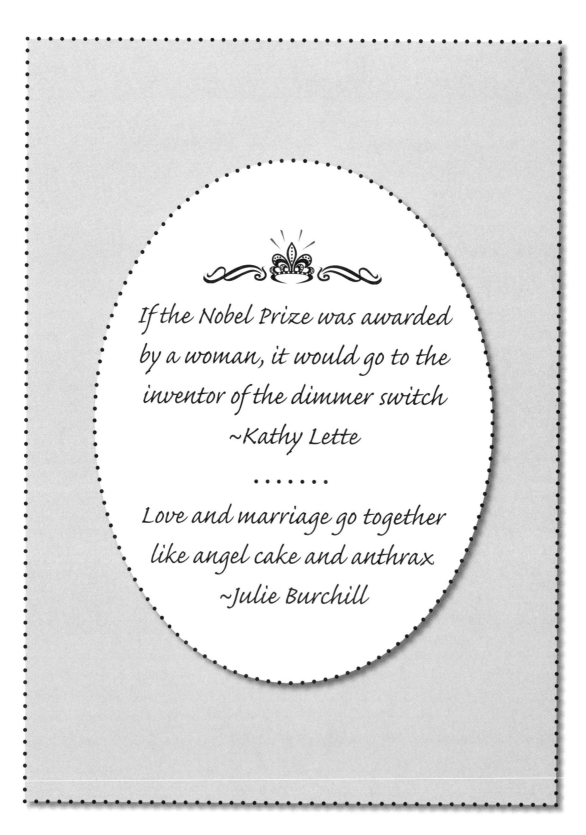

If the Nobel Prize was awarded by a woman, it would go to the inventor of the dimmer switch
~Kathy Lette

. . . .

Love and marriage go together like angel cake and anthrax
~Julie Burchill

Tiramisu Toffee Trifle Pie

* * * * *

I would gladly crawl across the Gobi Dessert
on hands and knees for a piece of this.

1 ½	Tbs. instant coffee	½	Cup powdered sugar
¾	Cup warm water	½	Cup chocolate syrup
1	Pound cake (large – frozen) – thawed	1	12 Oz. whipped topping
1	8 Oz. Mascarpone cheese or cream cheese	2	1.4 Oz. English toffee candy bars – crushed (Heath)

Stir coffee and ¾ cup warm water until coffee is dissolved. Cool. Cut cake into 14 slices. Then cut each slice in half diagonally. Place triangle in bottom and up sides of 9" deep dish pie plate. Drizzle coffee mixture over cake. Beat mascarpone cheese, sugar, and chocolate syrup at medium speed with mixer until smooth. Add 2 ½ C whipped topping and beat until light and fluffy. Spread evenly over cake. Dollop remaining whipped topping around edges. Sprinkle with crushed candy bars. Chill 8 hours.

Chocolate Angel Food Dessert

* * * * *

Always my requested birthday cake –
anything chocolate, delicate and delicious!

1	Angel food cake mix
2 Tbs.	Cocoa
2 Tbs.	Sugar

Add cocoa and sugar to dry mix. Prepare according to package directions and bake.

When cool, slice through twice making three sections. Melt one GIANT almond Hershey Chocolate Bar over hot water in double boiler. Cool. Beat one pint whipping cream until stiff. Fold chocolate bar into whipped cream. Frost between two layers and completely cover exterior of cake. Place in refrigerator or freezer at least 24 hours.

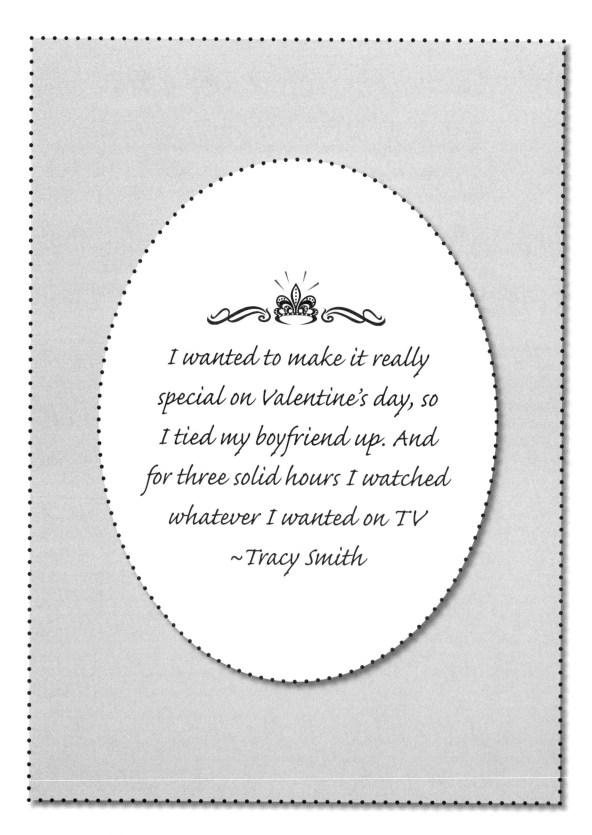

I wanted to make it really special on Valentine's day, so I tied my boyfriend up. And for three solid hours I watched whatever I wanted on TV
~Tracy Smith

Fresh Strawberries in Amaretto

* * * * *

From one of my sophisticated friends

2 Pints	Fresh strawberries – hulled & quartered
¼-½ C	Amaretto
1 -8 Oz.	Cream cheese
½ C	Sugar
2 Tbs.	Cream
¼ C	Amaretto

Cover strawberries with Amaretto and refrigerate. Combine remaining ingredients in a food processor and blend. Chill. If too thick, add a little more cream or liquor to desired consistency. When ready to serve, place strawberries in stemmed goblet and pour cream sauce over. Serve immediately.

Quick Fruit Topping

* * * * *

Light, refreshing and purely pleasurable.
When enough needs nothing more.

1 C	Sour cream
¼ C	Coconut
1 Jar	Macadamia nuts – chopped
¼ C	Apricot preserves

Combine above ingredients, chill and serve over fresh fruit.

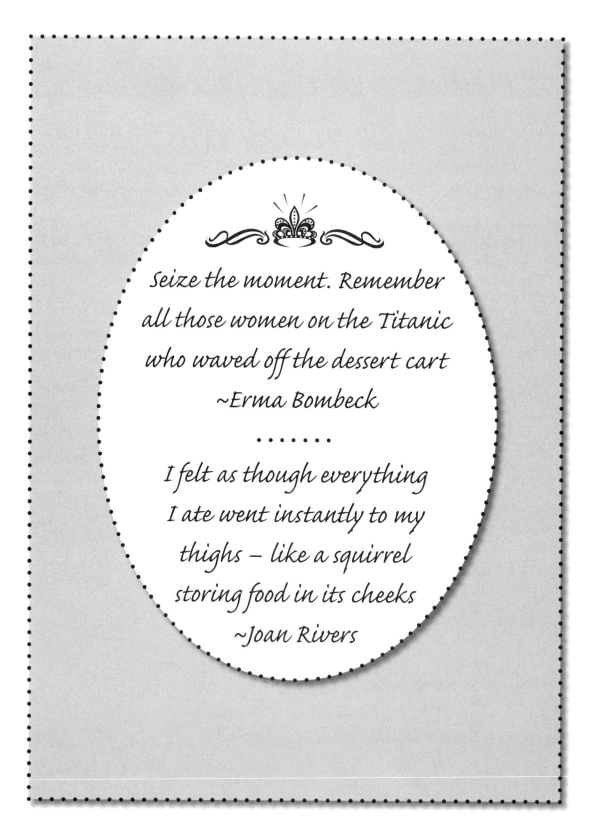

Seize the moment. Remember all those women on the Titanic who waved off the dessert cart
~Erma Bombeck

. . . . . .

I felt as though everything I ate went instantly to my thighs – like a squirrel storing food in its cheeks
~Joan Rivers

New York Cheesecake

* * * * *

It's so nice to have a man around the house! Particularly one who will make this dessert. Thanks Herb, for your favorite recipe

Crust:

1 ½ Cups Graham cracker crumbs	6 Tbs. butter – melted
	¼ Cup sugar

Combine ingredients and pat into a 9 or 10 inch spring form pan. Be sure to bring crumbs up sides a bit. Freeze for 10 minutes.

Cake:

2 Lb.'s creamed cheese	1 Tsp. vanilla
¾ Cup sugar	2 Tbs. cornstarch
2 Eggs – large & well beaten	1 Cup sour cream
	½ Tsp. orange or lemon zest

Heat oven to 400 and place pan of water in bottom of oven while cheesecake is baking. Beat sugar and cheese. Add in eggs, vanilla and cornstarch while beating. Stir in sour cream and citrus choice. Bake for 45 minutes. Turn off oven and let cake cool while in oven slightly propped open with wooden spoon. Leave cake in oven for three hours, then chill before enjoying.

Georgia Pecan Pie

* * * * *

A classic favorite – nothing but pure sin.

1 Prepared unbaked pie crust	6 Tbs. butter – melted & cooled
¾ Cup dark brown sugar – firmly packed	2 Tbs. molasses
3 Lg. eggs	1 Tsp. vanilla
½ Cup light corn syrup	2 Cups pecans – toasted & coarsely chopped

Whisk brown sugar, eggs, corn syrup, butter, molasses and vanilla to blend in a medium bowl. Stir in pecans. Pour filling into your prepared pie crust. Bake until filling is set and crust is deep golden brown, about 40 minutes at 350.

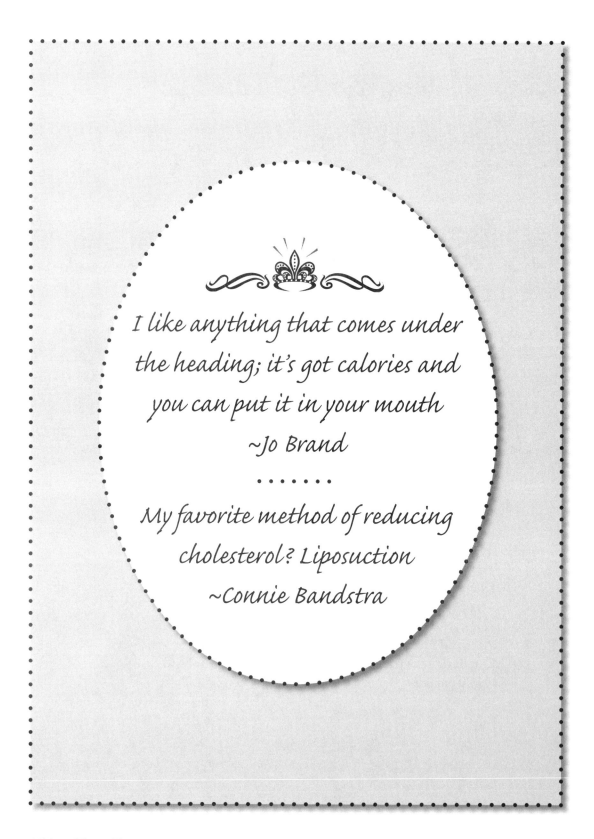

*I like anything that comes under
the heading; it's got calories and
you can put it in your mouth*
~Jo Brand

. . . .

*My favorite method of reducing
cholesterol? Liposuction*
~Connie Bandstra

Death By Chocolate
* * * * *

Our "Signature Dessert" and truly a thigh rubbing, magic wand waving experience! I get to be the fairy godmother and wave the magic wand, taking away all of your calories while you dine on this in the Tearoom!

1	Duncan Hines Dark Fudge Cake	1	Jar caramel ice cream topping (any brand)
1	Can Eagle Brand Condensed milk		

Mix and bake cake according to package directions. Pour into a 10" spring form pan that has been prepared. Bake according to directions. While hot, poke holes all over hot cake. Pour condensed milk over cake then cover with caramel topping. Let this mixture soak into cake. Cool and chill for 24 hours. Whip 1 pint whipping cream till stiff. Add 2 Tbs. sugar and vanilla. Frost top and sides of cake. Dust with Droste cocoa.

Peanut Butter Pie
* * * * *

If the ladies on "Survivor" will strip down for chocolate and peanut butter, I'm there as well. This pie is to be savored slowwwwwwly, one bite at a time.

1	Cup Graham cracker crumbs	2	8 Oz. cream cheese – room temp.
¼	Cup light brown sugar – firmly packed	2	Tbs. butter – melted
¼	Cup butter – melted	2	Tsp. vanilla
2	Cups creamy peanut butter	1 ½	Cups whipping cream
2	Cups sugar	4	Oz. semi-sweet chocolate
		3	Tbs. + 2 Tsp. hot coffee

Combine crumbs, brown sugar and ¼ C butter. Press into bottom and halfway up sides of 9-inch springform pan. Beat peanut butter, sugar, cream cheese, 2 Tbs. butter and vanilla in large bowl of an electric mixer until smooth and creamy. Beat cream until soft peaks form. Fold whipped cream into peanut butter mixture. Spoon into crust. Refrigerate 6 hours. Melt chocolate with coffee in double boiler over gently simmering water. Spread atop filling. Refrigerate until firm.

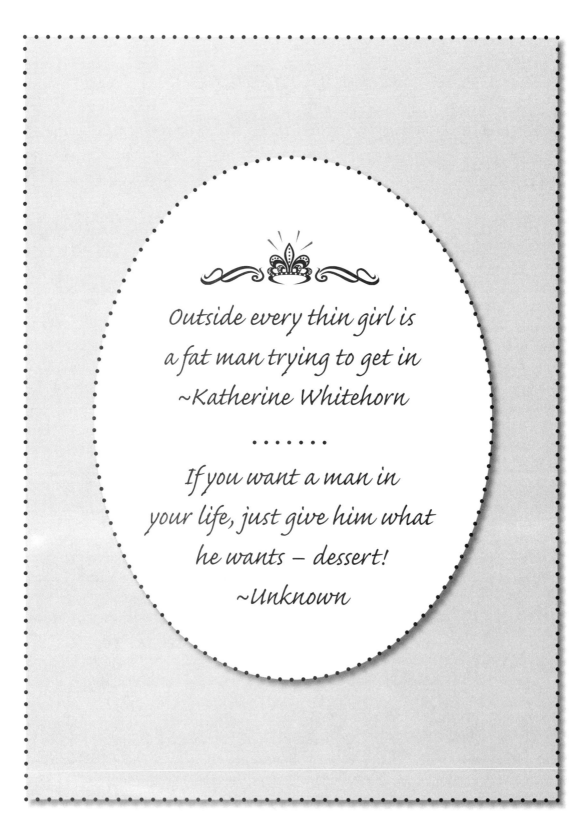

*Outside every thin girl is
a fat man trying to get in
~Katherine Whitehorn*

. . . .

*If you want a man in
your life, just give him what
he wants – dessert!
~Unknown*

Key Lime Pie

* * * * *

Close your eyes, feel the breeze and let this tickle your taste buds.

1 ½ C	Pecans – chopped
¾ C	Graham cracker crumbs
2	Limes – grated peeling
¾ Tsp.	Cinnamon
1 ½ Tbs.	Sugar
2 -14 Oz.	Cans sweetened condensed milk
7	Egg yolks
½ C	Key lime or other lime juice
2	Limes – grated peeling
	Whipped cream

Melt butter in medium skillet. Add pecans and sauté until lightly browned and toasted. Immediately remove nuts and butter from pan and place in food processor. Add crumbs, lime peel, cinnamon, sugar and mix with crumbs. Turn into 10" pie plate, reserving 2 ounces of crumbs for garnish. Evenly distribute crumb mixture over bottom, and up sides of pie plate, pressing to cover surface with the crust. Let rest at room temperature until ready to fill.

Filling: Beat egg yolks at high speed until smooth, 4 to 5 minutes. Slowly add condensed milk while mixer is running, but do not over-mix. Scrape down sides of bowl. Slowly add lime juice at medium speed. Add grated peel and continue to mix slowly. Pour into prepared pecan crust, smoothing top with spatula. Fill baking pan halfway with hot water and place on lowest rack of oven. Place pie plate on rack above water and bake at 300 until filling is firm to touch, 20 to 25 minutes. Do not allow pie to brown. Remove pie from oven and place on wire rack to cool. Place in refrigerator to set and chill about 4 hours. To serve, top pie with thick layer of whipped cream and sprinkle with reserved graham cracker crumbs.

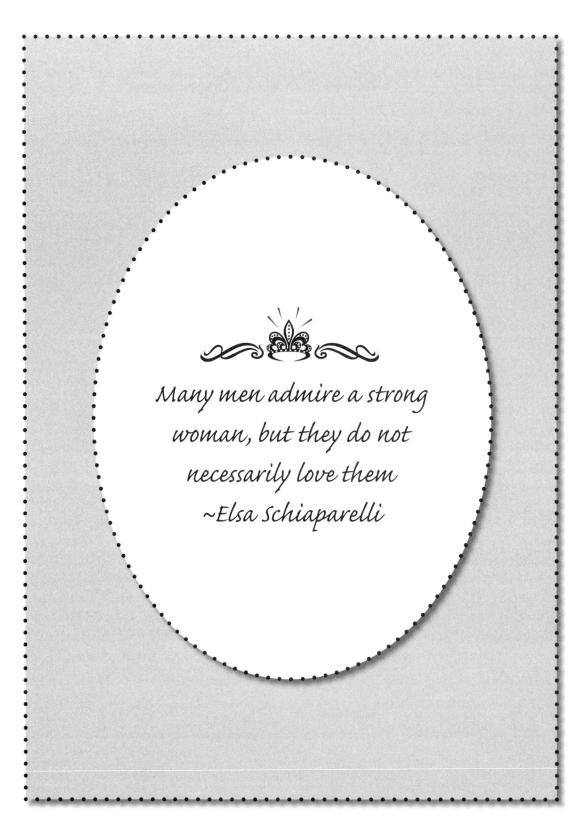

Many men admire a strong woman, but they do not necessarily love them

~Elsa Schiaparelli

Apple-Pecan Upside-Down Cake

* * * * *

Simply another favorite oral gratification and a home run winner!

1 -2 Oz. Pkg.	Chopped pecans
¼ C	Butter
1 C	Light brown sugar
2	Granny Smith apples – peeled, cored & sliced

Cake:	
1 C	Flour
2 Tsp.	Baking powder
½ Tsp.	Cinnamon
¼ Tsp.	Salt
6 Tbs.	Butter
¾ C	Sugar
1	Egg
½ Tsp.	Vanilla
6 Tbs.	Milk or cream – optional

Topping:

Toast pecans at 450 until lightly browned, about 10 minutes. Melt butter in small saucepan. Add brown sugar and cook, stirring until melted. Be certain to watch as sugar burns easily. Pour butter-sugar mixture into 9 inch round cake pan and spread to coat the bottom. Sprinkle chopped pecans on top of butter-sugar mixture. Place apples in concentric circles (slightly overlapping) over pecans.

Cake:

Sift flour, baking powder, cinnamon and salt into a bowl. Beat butter until light and fluffy. Add sugar and continue to beat 3-5 minutes. Add egg and vanilla and continue to beat until incorporated. Reduce speed; add flour mixture and milk, alternating. Continue to mix only until dry ingredients are completely mixed in. Spoon cake batter over topping and spread carefully so batter is even. Bake at 325 degrees until tester comes out clean, about 55 minutes. Cool in pan. Carefully run spatula around edge of pan and let stand another 10 to 15 minutes. Invert pan over large plate and let stand about 3 minutes. Serve warm with fresh whipped cream.

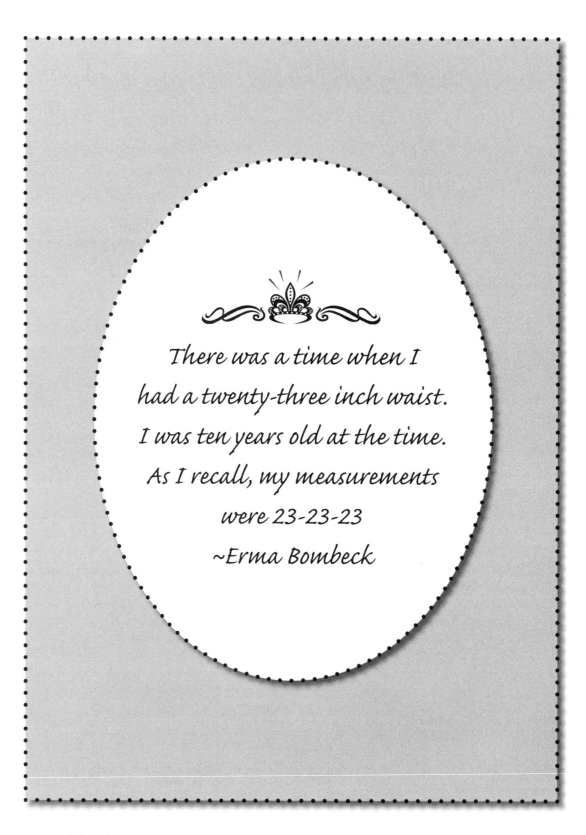

There was a time when I
had a twenty-three inch waist.
I was ten years old at the time.
As I recall, my measurements
were 23-23-23

~Erma Bombeck

Bananas Foster Bread Pudding

* * * * *

Light my fire – Light my fire – Light my fire--ooooooooh

1 Loaf	French bread – crumbled
1 ½ C	Whole milk
1 ½ C	Whipping cream
1 C	Banana liqueur
2 C	Sugar
½ C	Butter – melted
4	Eggs
2 Tbs.	Vanilla
5	Bananas – cut up
1 C	Chopped pecans
1 Tbs.	Ground cinnamon
	Bananas foster sauce

Prepare a 9x13 baking dish. Whisk milk, cream, liqueur, sugar, butter and eggs along with vanilla in large mixing bowl. Cut up bananas and toss with pecans and cinnamon.

Layer French bread, then banana mix, topping with French bread. Pour liquid mixture over all and press the bread down with back of a large mixing spoon to soak all bread. Bake in 350 oven for 60 minutes or until pudding is set and knife comes out clean.

Sauce:

½ C	Butter
2 C	Dark brown sugar
½ C	Banana liqueur
½ C	Dark rum
	Ground cinnamon

Melt butter in skillet. Stir in brown sugar to form creamy paste. Caramelize over medium heat 5 minutes. Stir in banana liquor and rum. Heat and ignite. Agitate to keep flame burning and add a few dashes of cinnamon to flame. Let flames die and serve warm over warm bread pudding. Makes 16 to 20 servings. Sauce can be served over bread pudding or ice cream.

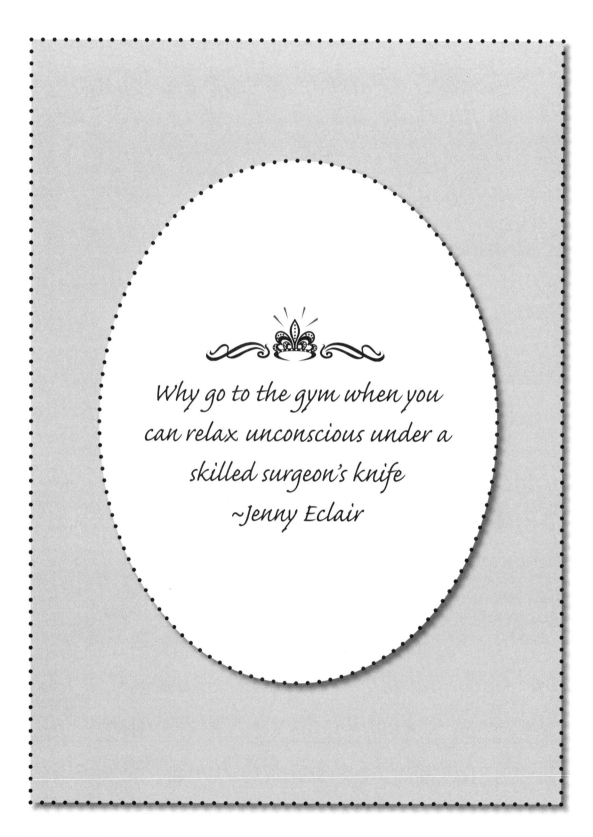

Why go to the gym when you can relax unconscious under a skilled surgeon's knife

~Jenny Eclair

Chocolate Bread Pudding with Bourbon-Pecan Caramel Sauce

* * * * *

Dessert Anyone??? You will be the High Priestess tonight and he'll be your slave when this is the after dinner delight.

Sauce:

1 ¼ C	Sugar
½ C	Water
¼ C	Corn syrup
1 Tbs.	Fresh lemon juice
1 ¼ C	Whipping cream
1 C	Pecans – chopped & toasted
2 Tbs.	Bourbon

Pudding:

2 C	Whole milk
2 C	Whipping cream
1 C	Sugar
8 Oz.	Semi-sweet chocolate – chopped
8 Lg.	Eggs
1 Tbs.	Vanilla
1 -1Lb.	Unsliced egg bread – crusts trimmed & cut into 1" pieces

For sauce: Stir sugar and water in heavy large saucepan over medium heat until sugar dissolves. Mix in corn syrup and lemon juice. Increase heat and boil without stirring until syrup turns deep amber, brushing down sides of pan with wet pastry brush and swirling pan occasionally. Remove from heat. Pour in cream (mixture will bubble up). Stir over low heat until caramel is melted and smooth. Increase heat; boil until sauce is reduced to 1 ⅔ cups, stirring often, about 4 minutes. Remove from heat. Mix in pecans and bourbon.

For pudding: Preheat oven to 350. Combine milk, cream and sugar in heavy large saucepan over medium-high heat. Stir until sugar dissolves and mixture comes to boil. Remove from heat. Add chocolate and stir until smooth. Beat eggs and vanilla in large bowl to blend. Gradually whisk in chocolate mixture. Add bread cubes. Let stand until bread absorbs some of custard, stirring occasionally, about 30 minutes. Transfer mixture to 9x13 inch glass baking dish. Cover with foil. Bake until set, about 45 minutes. Serve pudding warm or at room temperature with warm sauce.

Wedding cake – a food that
greatly reduces the sex drive
~Unknown

Caramel Ice Cream Cake

* * * * *

Just inject my veins with sugar, fat, and carbs.

1 -1 Lb.	Pound cake – thawed
2 Pints	Dulce De Leche ice cream (Haagen-Daz Brand) – slightly softened
1 -7 Oz. Jar	Marshmallow creme
½ Cup	Butterscotch caramel topping (Mrs. Richardson's)
4	English toffee bars – chopped

Cut pound cake into ⅓" thick slices. Halve each diagonally, forming triangles. Line the bottom of a 9" spring form pan with cake by arranging some triangles (points facing in) around bottom edge of pan. Fill in center with more cake triangles. Then cut additional pieces to fill in any remaining spaces. Spread 1 pint softened ice cream over cake. Cover with plastic and freeze until firm; about 1 hour.

Spread ¾ jar of marshmallow creme on top; save rest for another use. Sprinkle with ½ the chopped toffee bars and press them slightly with hand. Cover and freeze again for 30 minutes. Repeat, layering with remaining cake and softened ice cream. Freeze another 30 minutes. Top with caramel sauce, spreading to the edges, and the rest of the candy , pressing again with your hand to make sure it adheres. Cover tightly with plastic wrap and freeze until ice cream is set, at least 1 hour. (Can be prepared and frozen several days ahead of time.) To serve, remove pan sides and bottom of pan. Place cake on cutting board. With a sharp knife, cut wedges of cake, wiping knife between slices to make it easier to cut.

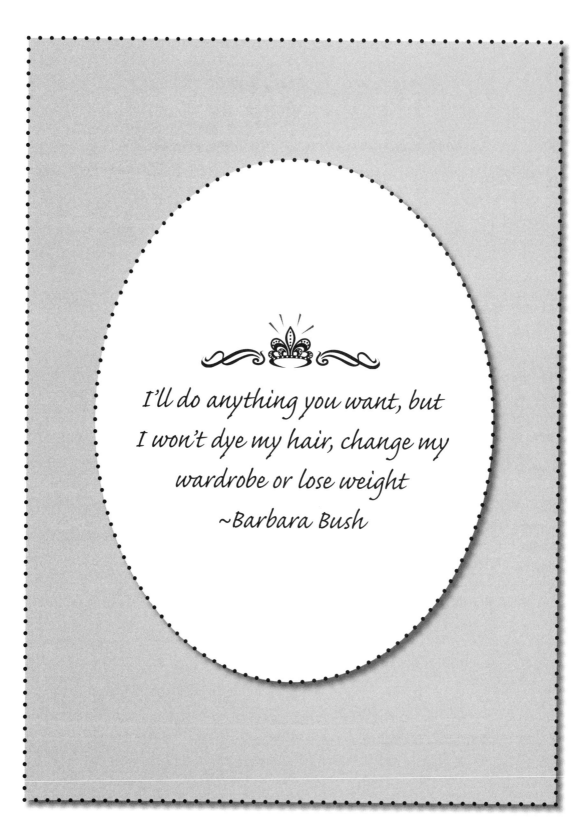

I'll do anything you want, but I won't dye my hair, change my wardrobe or lose weight
~Barbara Bush

Bread Pudding

* * * * *

Young and old will love this favorite old standby treat.
The ecstasy is in the topping.

5	Egg yolks
5	Whole eggs
1 C	Sugar
1 ½ Qt.	Heavy cream
1 Tsp.	Vanilla
½ Tsp.	Cinnamon
	Stale croissants – torn
	(enough to fill 9x12 baking dish)

Whisk together custard and set aside. Fill 9x12 pan with bread cubes. Pour custard over the bread and push down on bread so it gets soaked. Sprinkle with cinnamon/sugar mixture over the top if desired. Bake at 350 for 30-40 minutes till pudding is set. It will be jiggly, but not liquid. If the top gets too brown, cover with foil.

Creme Anglaise

½ Tbs.	Vanilla
2 C	Whipping cream
1 C	Milk
8	Egg yolks
½ C	Sugar

Combine all ingredients in saucepan and scald. Stir constantly, until sauce coats back of spoon. Cool to room temperature before refrigerating.

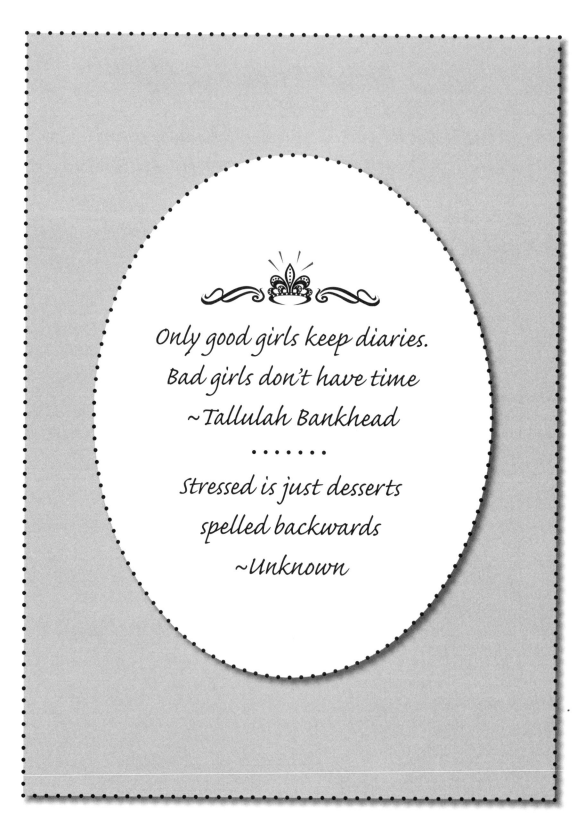

Only good girls keep diaries.
Bad girls don't have time
~Tallulah Bankhead

. . . .

Stressed is just desserts
spelled backwards
~Unknown

Apricot or Strawberry Torte
* * * * *

The doves are cooing and love is in the air when this is served for dessert!

1	Graham cracker pie shell (may use store prepared)	1 ⅓	Cups powdered sugar
1	Cup pecan halves	3	Eggs
½	Pt. whipping cream	1	#2 Can apricots, drained and snipped into small pieces. Or, sliced strawberries
1	Cup butter		

Cream butter, adding powdered sugar gradually and beating thoroughly. Add eggs one at a time and beat well after each addition. Spread butter mixture over crust. Top with either apricots or fresh strawberries. Top with nuts. Spread with whipped cream. Sprinkle on buttered graham crumbs. Refrigerate for 12 hours.

Texas Sheet Cake
* * * * *

Chocolate is so sensual – he'll think you are in the mood!

2	Cups flour	**Frosting:**	
2	Cups sugar	½	Cup butter
½	Tsp. salt	5	Tbs. milk
1	Tsp. baking soda	4	Tbs. cocoa
2	Eggs	1	1Lb. box powdered sugar
1	Cup sour cream	1	Tsp. vanilla
1	Cup butter		
1	Cup water		
6	Tbs. cocoa (rounded!!!!)		

Combine flour, sugar, salt, soda, eggs and sour cream; set aside. In medium saucepan, bring butter, water and cocoa to a boil. Mix this into the flour mixture in two batches. Bake at 350 for 20 to 25 minutes.

Frosting: In saucepan, melt butter. Add milk and cocoa; bring to boil. Remove from heat; add powdered sugar and vanilla. Pour immediately over cake when it comes out of oven.

My dream is to die in a tub of
ice cream with Mel Gibson
~Joan Rivers

· · · · · · ·

Eat drink and be merry,
for tomorrow we diet
~Alice Thomas Ellis

Heavenly Brownies

* * * * *

You'll know there's a heaven after just one bite.

1 Box	Brownie mix – your favorite to make a 9x12
1 Jar	Marshmallow cream
1	Frosting recipe
Frosting:	Same ingredients as the Texas Sheet Cake

Bake brownies according to package directions. Upon removing from oven, spread marsh-mallow creme over brownies. Frost immediately. Sprinkle with nuts if desired.

Hershey Pie

* * * * *

Any left over whipped cream gets dabbed behind the ears!!!!

6 -1.35 Oz.	Hershey bars with almonds
16	Marshmallows
½ C	Milk
1 C	Whipping cream
1	Graham cracker pie shell

Melt Hershey candy bars and marshmallows in milk in top of double boiler. Cool thoroughly. Beat whipping cream until stiff. Fold whipped cream into chocolate. Pour into crust. Place in refrigerator until serving time for at least 3 hours.

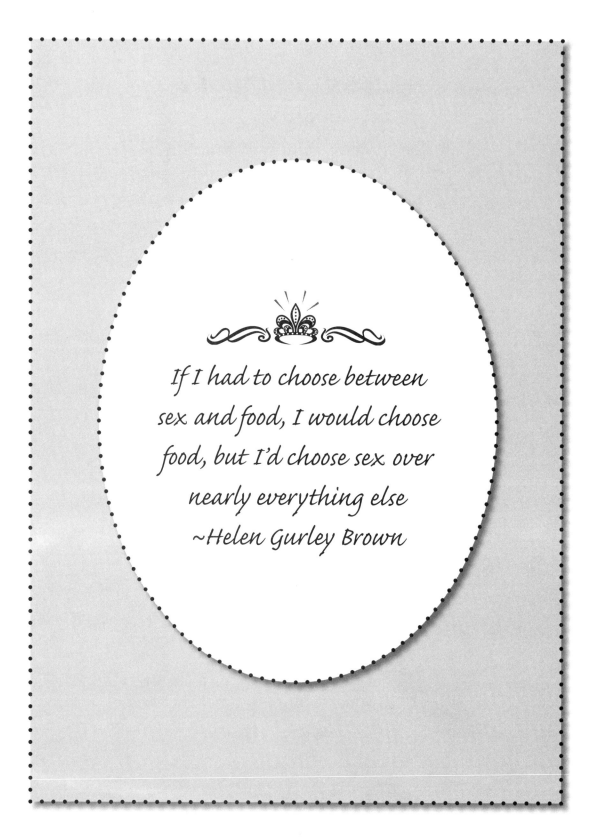

If I had to choose between sex and food, I would choose food, but I'd choose sex over nearly everything else
~Helen Gurley Brown

Million Dollar Pie

* * * * *

Where's my wand when I need it the most!

1 C	Sweetened condensed milk
½ C	Lemon juice
1 -9 Oz.	Whipped topping
½ C	Nuts
1 Can	Crushed pineapple – drained
1 Jar	Maraschino cherries – chopped
2	Graham cracker pie crusts

Combine condensed milk and lemon juice. Add whipped topping and the remaining ingredients. Pour into 2 graham cracker crusts. Must be refrigerated. Garnish with a few extra chopped cherries and nuts.

Derby Pie

* * * * *

Forget "that" race, you'll be the only filly getting chased around the house.

2 Lg.	Eggs
4 Tbs.	Bourbon
¼ C	Cornstarch
1 C	Sugar
½ C	Butter
1 C	Pecans – chopped
1 C	Chocolate bits
¾ C	Coconut

Combine eggs, bourbon, cornstarch, sugar and butter. Mix well, add pecans, chocolate bits and coconut. Pour into unbaked pie shell. Bake 33 to 35 minutes in preheated oven at 350. Warm before serving. Top with whipped cream.

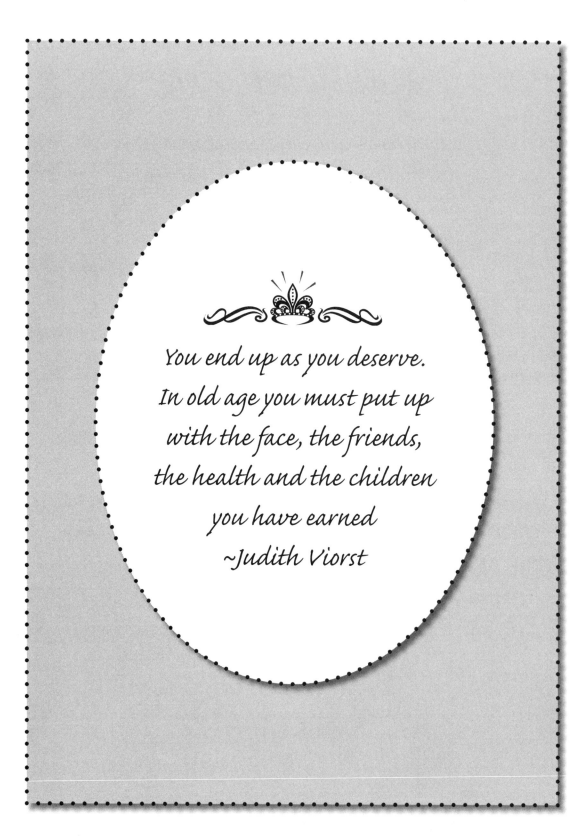

You end up as you deserve.
In old age you must put up
with the face, the friends,
the health and the children
you have earned
~Judith Viorst

Tasty Temptations

A Collection of Recipes Inspired by the World Famous Teacups & Tiaras

Published by:

Specific House PUBLISHING *Boston*

Specific House Publishing
Boston, MA

Requests for permission or for more information contact:

Connie Bandstra
Teacups & Tiaras
304 5th Street
West Des Moines, IA 50265

515-277-8400

www.TeacupsandTiaras.com

Printed in the United States of America

Cover design and text layout by: Ad Graphics, Inc., Tulsa, OK

ISBN 0-9674586-6-8

TASTY
TEMPTATIONS

A COLLECTION OF RECIPES INSPIRED BY THE WORLD FAMOUS
TEACUPS & TIARAS

Connie Bandstra

Specific
House
PUBLISHING
Boston